letter- a personal communication
open letter- a letter printed publicly as a matter of general interest and concern
letters- the world of literature, learning, readers and writers

Open Letters is a publishing house owned and run by women.
Our books are 'open letters' to our readers. They combine the warmth and
intimacy of exchanges between friends with the vigour of serious issues publicly
addressed. Our aim is to open up the world of Letters by producing books which
let in new or or unheard voices and ideas. We seek to bridge the gaps between
academic disciplines, between feminist theory and practice and between those
writing and reading within academic institutions and those outside.
Our books are intended for today's
Common Reader, in whose existence we firmly believe.

Tea and Leg-Irons

Caroline Gonda came to Scotland in 1989 to take up a lectureship in the English Department of the University of Dundee, where, amongst other things, she has set up an undergraduate course, "Women's Writing in the United States and Canada", and an extra-mural pilot course in Women's Studies, "Focus on Women". Her Ph.D. thesis for the University of Cambridge, "Fathers and Daughters in Novels from Eliza Haywood to Mary Brunton", was accepted in 1991 and she is currently working on a book based upon that research. The changes of perspective which took place as she became a consciously lesbian reader have prompted her present work on the relation between women's reading and sexuality.

Tea and Leg-Irons:

New Feminist Readings from Scotland

Edited by Caroline Gonda

OPEN LETTERS
LONDON 1992

First published by Open Letters,
147 Northchurch Road, London N1 3NT
1992

British Library Cataloguing-in-Publication Data
A Catalogue record for this book is available from
The British Library

ISBN 1 85789 000 0

Phototypeset in 10/11½ pt Baskerville
by Intype, London

Printed and bound in Great Britain by
BPCC Hazells Ltd
Member of BPCC Ltd

Contents

Illustrations

All figures drawn by Ann Blythe.

Acknowledgements

The cover illustration, "Miss Mary Blandy in Oxford Castle Goal [*sic*], charged with the Cruel Murder of her Father, Mr. Francis Blandy, late of Henley upon Thames in Oxfordshire, by Puting [*sic*] Poison into his Water Gruel, 1751", forms the frontispiece of a contemporary pamphlet, *A Genuine Account of the Most Horrid Parricide committed by Mary Blandy* . . . (printed and sold in Oxford and London, 1751), and is reproduced here by permission of the Syndics of Cambridge University Library. Mary Blandy is the subject of Caroline Gonda's essay, "Exactly Them Words: Histories of a Murderous Daughter".

Carol Anderson's essay, "Debateable Land: The Prose Work of Violet Jacob", is a revised version of a paper originally given at the Second International Literature of Region and Nation Conference, University of Nottingham, 1988.

Christine Crow's poem, "Cimetière Marin", which forms the first half of "A Voice Between The Bars?", also appears in *Paul Valéry: Musique, Mystique, Mathématique*, edited by Brian Stimpson and Paul Gifford and published by Presses Universitaires de Lille, 1992. It is printed here by kind permission of the editors and publishers.

In Alison Smith's essay, "How William Carlos Williams Gave Birth", all material quoted from *William Carlos Williams: The Collected Poems 1909–1939*, Volume 1, edited by A. Walton

Litz and Christopher MacGowan, Carcanet Press, Manchester, 1987, is reprinted here with the permission of Carcanet Press Ltd.

An Unabashedly Political Preface

The idea for this book dates back to a conversation I had with Alison Hennegan in October 1991. The news had just broken that the Government's Universities Funding Council (the UFC) had yet again brought forward the deadline for its Research Selectivity Exercise, the mechanism by which the universities' futures would be determined. As *The Higher* (formerly *The Times Higher Education Supplement*) noted in its lead story of 4th October, academics had been told only two months earlier that the deadline for submissions would be February 1993 (itself a revised deadline): now it was to be June 1992. With a wave of the Government's magic wand, books and articles scheduled for publication between June and February disappeared. Departments could not even claim credit for items in press as of June 1992, which would have appeared in time to meet the old (new) deadline, but were now disallowed by this latest outbreak of goalpost-moving.

We had watched those goalposts shift many times over the previous two years: it seemed sometimes as if hardly a month went by without some new directive, contradicting what had gone before. With this latest development, though, departments' attempts to work steadily and diligently towards improving their research performance and research rating were overturned. The move penalized departments for exercising prudence, making long-term plans: these traditional virtues clearly had no appeal for the Government which had once called for a return to Victorian values.

Perhaps, though, the values it had in mind were those of Dickens's Mr Gradgrind. The research measuring process certainly suggested a hostile scepticism about the worth (at times, it seemed, about the very existence) of anything which could not be quantified, reduced to statistics. Each member of a department was to submit two "mainstream" academic publications: books, essays in books, or articles in refereed, subject-based journals; and two "other" publications: reviews, dictionary entries, articles in journals not acceptable for the first category. (The hierarchy of refereed journals is nothing like as clear in the humanities as it is in the sciences – one of many instances in which the humanities would suffer, in this exercise, from having science criteria falsely applied to them.) Departments which could not field a full complement at least of "mainstream" publications were likely to suffer in the ratings. The insistence on counting departments' publications per head, rather than as a departmental whole, meant that there could be no compensatory offsetting of highly prolific staff members against those working on projects unlikely to result in quick publications (on scholarly editions of texts, for example); or against new, young staff, whose publishing careers were still ahead of them, and many of whom would still be completing Ph.D.s. Once again, long-term planning, whether by individuals working on substantial projects, or by departments appointing with an eye to the future, was being penalized.

With its insistence on quantity, the research measuring exercise favoured short-term results over long-term quality and – one might assume – articles over books. An article may be quicker to produce, it's true – but, in the humanities at any rate, it can take an unconscionable time to appear. (The misapplication of science criteria strikes again: in the sciences, articles really are the quickest way of getting your work into print.) Not only can a humanities journal routinely take more than six months to *reject* an article (whereupon the whole protracted process of submission and consideration has to begin again, because it's not done to submit the same piece to more than one journal at a time), but the lead time of journals is such that even an article *accepted*, with unusual rapidity, in three months, can still take up to two and a half years from submission to publication. (I speak from experience on both counts, but neither experience is uncommon.) For the humanities, then, this latest truncation of the review period was an unqualified disaster.

Most galling of all, perhaps, was an inescapable awareness of the political motives which kept those goalposts on the move: the Government's declared commitment to "expanding" higher education – with no additional expenditure to relieve lecture rooms already overcrowded, library facilities already overstretched, staff already overworked. The most recent attempt at expansion on the cheap had failed when universities, instructed to undercut each other with competitive bids for student course costs, had sensibly refused to bid below the Government's suggested "guide prices". Now, by abolishing the "binary divide" between universities and polytechnics, allowing polytechnics to apply for university status, a massive expansion of "university" education would take place at a stroke – and at no extra cost.

What this meant in terms of funding was that universities' and polytechnics' funding bodies would now be combined – but redivided into separate funding councils for England, Scotland, and Wales. These councils would take charge of allocating research funding: previously one-third of the universities' block grants, this funding would now be redistributed on the basis of *all* departments' ratings in the Research Selectivity Exercise. Departments would be rated from 1 to 5, with consequent gains in research funding for those scoring 4 or 5, and corresponding losses for those with lower scores. One UFC member quoted in *The Higher* warned that "non-laboratory departments with ones and twos in the research rating have had it next time round for all major research funding." Many saw this plan as likely to lead to a two- or three-tier university system, with universities classified as R (research only), R x T (research and teaching), and T (teaching only); the argument that research and teaching are interdependent, and that you can't do one properly without the other, fell on stony ground. As *The Higher* pointed out, it was in order to ensure that these new funding councils and processes were in place before a spring general election that the deadline had been brought forward yet again. Political expediency was calling the tune for the future of the universities.

It was in this context that the idea for *Tea and Leg-Irons* came into being, as I voiced my anger and frustration that, no matter how much publishable material I might have on the stocks, none of it could possibly see the light of day within the newly revised deadline. But so many feminist academics must be in the same situation, Alison said; especially since the most natural outlets for feminist scholarship were more likely to be classed as "other" than as "mainstream". These days, paradoxically, books could be published more quickly than articles: why shouldn't I edit a book of essays by feminist literary scholars working in Scottish universities, who, like me, had work ready for publication but not yet placed? The Scottish emphasis would be a useful reminder to English academics (who often seemed unaware of our existence) of the variety of interesting work being done in Scotland's university literature departments, much of it also concerned with Scottish topics. That Scottish focus would be an additional attraction for readers in continental Europe, traditionally more aware of, and interested in, Scotland as a country in its own right. For a publishing house looking towards Europe as its home market, that must surely be a bonus. What's more, by using material that was ready to go, and keeping to a tight production schedule, we could have the added satisfaction of seeing the book come out in June 1992 – in time to meet the deadline, benefit our respective departments, and cock a snook at the Government. The interest and shelf-life of the book would naturally be determined by its contents, not by the political context of its conception; but its *timing* could be a usefully political act.

The initial conception and impetus, then, came from Alison Hennegan, who also suggested that the book might be one of the first published by Open Letters. Ros de Lanerolle and Gillian Hanscombe, the other directors of Open Letters, were quick to see the possibilities of such a book, and generous in their support and encouragement of the project from start to finish. It would have been impossible for us to meet the necessarily tight production schedules without the enthusiastic support of Alice McIlroy, who cheerfully undertook to copy-edit the volume over Christmas and New Year; or without Alison Hennegan's stamina as in-house editor and her insistence on maintaining standards while working against the clock.

Opening Remarks

"Tea and Leg-Irons" was originally my affectionate short-hand for the picture reproduced on the cover of this book, in which a woman is seen performing an apparently safe and familiar, genteel and domestic action – taking tea with a guest – but is doing so in a startling and unfamiliar context: in prison, and in shackles. The picture is not only a supposedly authentic portrait of one particular eighteenth-century woman, but also offers a haunting and shocking image which carries a wider meaning for feminist critics. Tea has so many resonances and associations for women: once a luxury, now a staple; remedy for shock, or well earned rest; practical or dainty; essential and trivial; relied on and taken for granted. Tea, as in "over the teacups"; "tea and sympathy"; "a little tea, a little chat"; "a storm in a teacup"; "reading the tea-leaves". From the Japanese tea ceremony to the eighteenth-century daughter seen in our cover picture, making tea is a traditionally feminine activity. Dispensing tea, dispensing hospitality, may seem a proprietorial or enfreeing act on the part of the woman performing it. As an intrinsically domestic activity laid down as feminine, however, it is in fact confining. The bars on the window were always metaphorically there for the eighteenth-century daughter – and for her successors. The leg-irons, apparently so out of place, suggest the reality of shackles below that smoothly decorous and hospitable appear-

ance; they recall feminism's traditional awareness of the colli-
sion – and sometimes the identity – between violent confinement and everyday domesticity.

The particular relevance of this jarring image for us as
feminist scholars and critics lies in our need to be aware of
the many ways in which we, too, could be shackled or confined
(including getting stuck with pouring out the tea), and in our
need to resist these confinements, whatever forms they may
take. Feminists have fought to get into the academy, and
fought again to get women's issues on to the academic agenda,
whether in the revision of traditional courses (redefining the
syllabus) or in the provision of separate space (establishing
Women's Studies); and the fight is not over yet. Having bat-
tled our way into the institutions, though, we must take care
not to get locked into institutional thinking. This includes
resisting those developments within the academy which
exclude feminists outside it.

This double perspective of locking out and locking in is
especially useful and appropriate for a volume coming out of
Scotland. Scotland has long been both locked into and locked
out of the English political and economic systems, its resources
swallowed up without acknowledgement. This process extends
to Scottish culture, too. An Oxford graduate in English
shocked a friend of mine by asking, "What Scottish literature
is there, apart from Burns?" – and was shocked in return
when she reeled off a list including David Hume, James
Boswell, Susan Ferrier, James Hogg, Thomas Carlyle, Robert
Louis Stevenson, Margaret Oliphant, George MacDonald,
J.M. Barrie, John Buchan, and Muriel Spark. It wasn't that
he hadn't heard of them: he knew them all, admired many of
them, was a passionate fan of Boswell; yet he had managed
to blank out their Scottishness. Literature in English which
gets taken seriously by the academy becomes "English literature"; Scottishness becomes invisible when it suits English
readers. Tobias Smollett – another author this man hadn't
realized was Scottish – would not have been surprised, though.
This is what he had to say on the subject in 1771:

> If the truth must be told, the South Britons in general
> are wofully ignorant in this particular. What between

want of curiosity and traditional sarcasms, the effect of ancient animosity, the people at the other end of the island know as little of Scotland as of Japan.[1]

The implied exoticism of Scotland for the "South Britons" in Smollett's remark brings us to another aspect of locking out and locking in: the question of language and of whether, when dealing with literature written in Scots, to gloss or not to gloss. Should we impose a false exoticism on Scots words, thereby alienating many Scottish readers from their own familiar language; or should we leave passages in Scots unglossed, risking comprehension problems for non-Scottish readers (not just for English ones)? In the end we adopted a consistent principle of glossing, not only between Scots and English, but also (in Valerie Allen's piece) between mediaeval and modern English. Specialist terms and items of information have also been glossed: any specialists thinking of standing on their dignity about this should please remember that, as often as not, they too become amateurs once they step 150 years out of their own periods. For those readers who are amateurs across the whole range, we have done our best to remove unnecessary impediments from the path, whether by supplying additional information in notes, or by incorporating it into the pieces themselves.

In its assumption of a non-specialist readership, this volume goes against the academic defeatism – or hubris – which assumes that only three or four other experts will ever read one's work anyway, and that therefore general explanations are redundant, if not positively offensive. The reverse of this argument is the other, equally widespread assumption that general readers don't want to know all the dry, boring details of a subject, and that therefore a book for the general reader mustn't clutter itself up with scholarly apparatus. But all readers, whether general or specialist, have a right to the information which will enable them to find out more about a subject, should they wish to do so. These assumptions about what the general reader wants or doesn't want, about who does or doesn't read writing by academics, all too easily lead to exclusive, closed writing; to barring the door against non-specialist readers instead of opening it to let them in. One of the many disadvantages of such a closed system is that it leads to falling standards. Bibliography and other kinds of scholarly apparatus are seen as a matter of institutional regulations or "house style". This leads to the dangerous minimalism of doing what's required rather than what's needed – and to confusing the two. *The MHRA Handbook*, one of the recommended guides for postgraduate students, makes no provision for including publishers' names in references and bibliographical material; some academic publishers have even told authors that they were not allowed to include this information. Once again the assumption seems to be that anybody who matters will have easy access to a copyright library (not the case even for most academics) and therefore won't need the information; and that anybody who doesn't matter isn't likely to be interested anyway.

This confusion seems to come from a false equation of academics and scholars, academics and intellectuals – and from an equally false idea of professionalization. The conventions and requirements of academic publishing (themselves increasingly dictated by budgetary rather than scholarly considerations) take on the force of laws. In this "publish or perish" climate, where publication becomes an end in itself rather than a means of communicating one's research, it often seems easier just to do as you're told.

The issue of giving adequate information, rather than just meeting requirements, is an important one for feminists, however, given the enforced invisibility and disenfranchisement of the independent feminist scholar, unattached to any institution. At a meeting in 1990 of the Northern Network – a loosely knit association of women working on English literature – one woman who had recently retired from an academic post said that she had felt unable to update her entry for the Network Register because she felt she "wasn't anything any more". Other women without academic jobs voiced similar feelings. The question here, one which recurs at different points throughout this volume, is the question of where value resides and who determines it: who decides who (and what) matters? There is a danger that the price of coming in out of the cold, into the institution, is being asked to adopt the institution's ways and values, to leave your unsuitable, less well educated or less fortunate sisters at the door. This process perpetuates the institution's self-set, artificially high value, through those who have best reason to be suspicious of it.

As Jane Marcus usefully reminds us, however, the institutional past is not an undifferentiated mass of villainy, evil practices, and male academics using their various skills to write women out of history: "without the survival of these skills [bibliography, editing, textual scholarship, biography, and literary history] and the appropriation of them, women will again lose the history of their own culture."[2] These skills, too, are part of our heritage; we shut ourselves off from them at our peril. The pieces gathered here, far from severing or denying links with the past, identify and acknowledge connections between apparently disparate authors, places, works, and traditions.

This volume brings together contributors from a wide variety of different backgrounds (Scottish, Irish, and English), and working on a variety of different subjects: mediaeval to 1990s; Scottish, English, French, North American – both us and Canadian; poetry, fiction, and pamphlet literature. The critical approaches used are equally varied, from conventional literary history to recent feminist and gender theory. Some of the critics writing here become themselves the subjects of criticism. Margaret Elphinstone uses the experience of writing fiction to illuminate her treatment of contemporary feminist fantasy in the Scottish literary tradition; and Christine Crow's work is itself the subject of an essay by Mary Orr. Our aim, to borrow a phrase from Mary Orr's title, is that of "crossing divides" – bridging unhelpful gaps between subject areas and schools of criticism, as well as between "academic" and "non-academic" readers.

The collection begins with Dorothy Porter McMillan's essay, "Writers and Heroines", tracing the development of Scottish women's writing over two hundred years. She shows the changes in women's attitudes to their own writing, from the early writers' self-effacement and avoidance of publicity, through a painful ambivalence between pride and shame in authorship, to the emergence of a more relaxed, less threatened self-consciousness. Her essay also brings out the challenges and examples these writers offer present-day feminists: the question – still hotly debated by feminist critics and theorists – of whether women should speak with a specifically gendered voice; or the proof, in the unembarrassed didacticism of the earlier writers, that art and ethics can fight on the same side, need not be opposed.

Whereas McMillan explores connections and continuities over a wide chronological span of Scottish women's writing, Carol Anderson's essay on Violet Jacob suggests the range and variety which can exist within the work of one writer. Violet Jacob is usually defined as a regional poet; in fact, Anderson argues, her very diversity as a novelist and short-story writer; as an author of children's books, family history, and diaries; and as a visual artist, is one of the factors which has prevented her from being taken seriously. Another is her failure to fit neatly into a reductive and defensive (male) idea of Scottishness. Anderson points out "the need for a criticism of Scottish literature which is open to the potentialities of work done by writers with varying interests and with varying attitudes to their homeland." Her essay, exploring the many different meanings of "debateable land" (including the meaning of a land where debate is alive and well), notes Violet Jacob's own ability to lay imaginative claim to her territory, her "own country".

Margaret Elphinstone's essay shows contemporary Scottish women writers laying imaginative claim to a somewhat different territory. This is the land of traditional ballads, where strong women move in "a world that is both fantastic, and subject to practical and domestic details". It is also, though, the interior world of madness and of the divided self – the classic themes of Scottish literary fantasy. Elphinstone stresses the advantages, for contemporary Scottish women writers, of maintaining connection with that fantasy tradition, which constantly requires its readers "to go beyond the fragmentation of language, nationality, and culture, and to read the unstated narrative." Through their use of fantasy, as she demonstrates, those women writers direct attention to the spaces and silences "within the bounds of patriarchy or the assumptions of a dominant group", making readers aware of what, in those contexts, cannot be said.

My own essay, on the eighteenth-century parricide, Mary Blandy, explores different kinds of female confinement and enclosure, through the constraints of decorum as well as through literal imprisonment. The many "histories" of Mary Blandy, produced at a time when "history" was as likely to mean "fiction" as "true story", are overlaid by a grid of eighteenth-century ideas about relations between fathers and daughters: the patterns thus set up impose their own constraints, with nature imitating art as well as vice versa. For contemporary readers, however, these familiar patterns would have offered comfort in the face of a shocking domestic murder. The essay also touches on a piece of eighteenth-century history often reduced (as Jane Goldman's essay reminds us) to a romantic story: the Jacobite Rebellion of 1745, reverberations of which were felt in many unexpected ways.

Flora Alexander's essay on mothers and daughters in the fiction of Alice Munro offers a more delicate and subtle range of negotiations between parent and child than Mary Blandy's arsenic in the water-gruel. As Alexander points out, the mother–daughter relationship has been a growing preoccupation of twentieth-century women writers. In this volume, Sian Hayton's female giants, discussed in Margaret Elphinstone's essay, provide an interesting contrast to Munro's daughter figures. The price of the giant daughters' magical power is that their mothers, mortal women impregnated by the giant father, must die in giving birth to them. For the daughters in Munro's work, coming to terms with the mother's death is the process by which they learn and accept their own place in the world. Where the mothers are still living, the question of what to accept or reject from their offered maternal inheritance is still a pressing one – as it is, in a more metaphorical sense, for feminists engaging with the past, thinking back (as Virginia Woolf put it) through our mothers.

Unusual varieties of birth and creation appear in the next two essays, both of which observe and comment upon the male artist at work. Valerie Allen, in her essay on Chaucer's

The Merchant's Tale, shows the significance of the myths of Pygmalion and Narcissus for mediaeval theories of artistic creation, and for woman's place in those theories. Her essay also examines some unsuccessful mediaeval attempts to enclose women and their speech, from the unstoppable mystic, Margery Kempe, via Chaucer's Wife of Bath, to the adulterous May of *The Merchant's Tale*, with her quick-witted and ingenious exculpation. The presence of this essay in the volume represents another kind of opening up; the decision to include a mediaeval piece despite the difficulty of the language. (Help has been provided, though in fact the originals are not as difficult as they look, and are much more enjoyable than any prose translation, however good, could be – try reading aloud.)

Alison Smith's account of "How William Carlos Williams Gave Birth" provides a different view of male creativity and of a male artist's attempt to create life without the aid of a woman, to usurp women's power of giving birth. Williams's views on gender, which have hitherto received little attention, have important implications for his poetic theories, Smith argues. In particular, Williams's view of woman as at once more universal and more earthbound, more objective, than man, demands a reconsideration of his celebrated poetic principle, "No ideas but in things".

Jane Goldman's essay on Virginia Woolf also begins by examining metaphor and woman's relation to it. She goes on to look at the specifically Scottish and Hebridean references of Woolf's novel, *To the Lighthouse*, refusing to accept the traditional belief that (despite Woolf's many claims to the contrary) the novel is "really" set in Cornwall. Arguing that the Hebridean location provides "a sophisticated set of allusions which ground the feminist import of the work in a discourse of colonial metaphor", she insists that Woolf criticism must address what it has hitherto ignored, the "appropriateness of Scotland as a parallel with woman in relation to ruling metaphor". In the course of her essay she also offers a solution to one of the most obscure and abstract passages in *To the Lighthouse*. It is fitting that her essay appears in the section *Connections and Alliances*, in which hidden connections are brought to light, old alliances revived (including the Auld

Alliance itself, that centuries-old link between Scotland and France) and new ones forged.

Mary Orr's essay in this section shows how Christine Crow's novel, *Miss X, or the Wolf Woman* dismantles old categories of gender and genre, and sets up new connections between myths and texts from Ancient Egypt, Greek mythology and the Bible, to Freud's Wolf Man and Monique Wittig's *Le Corps Lesbien*. *Miss X*, Orr suggests, opens up the storehouses of myth to the keen gaze of the woman writer, who should no more reject their treasures than refuse to take her pitcher to *The Well of Loneliness*, or to be illumined by the lighthouse beams of the Woolf woman. It is important, however, that such pluralism does not degenerate into sloppiness or slackness: Orr stresses the intricate construction and connectedness of *Miss X*, which does not wolf its myths down indiscriminately, but incorporates them simultaneously into a critical framework and into a structure of fiction, coherent and imaginative as well as playful and self-conscious.

Christine Crow herself provides the final piece in the volume: a subversive, feminist re-reading of Paul Valéry's classic poem *Le Cimetière Marin* (The Graveyard by the Sea), set in the alternative "cimetière marin" of St Andrews. Here poetry itself functions as criticism, once again resisting the fragmentation of creative and critical. Her serious but playful commentary (mixed modes again) discusses what happens when Valéry's universal (male) poet is made to speak with a woman's voice, and warns that women writers should not shut themselves off from the power of that universal voice simply because it has been previously commandeered by men. While her poem recalls the continuing historical importance of the "Auld Alliance", the commentary suggests new and powerful alliances for feminist writing which, she asserts, must never rest content with "prising open old texts", but must seek to open up international boundaries (the Auld Alliance strengthened and expanded), to Open up the world of Letters itself.

Caroline Gonda
Dundee, New Year's Day 1992

Scottish Women Writers

Heroines and Writers

Dorothy Porter McMillan

The processes by means of which writing becomes central rather than peripheral to the lives of women writers may be observed with unusual clarity within the Scottish tradition. The journey of Scottish women writers from self-effacement to self-determination takes about two hundred years and can be characterized, in one of its aspects, as the movement from the heroine as writer to the writer as heroine.

Lady Grisell Baillie (1665–1746) was the first in the line of aristocratic songwriters whose approach to writing Mac-Diarmid characterized as *noblesse oblige.*[1] Her most famous production is the song "Werena my heart licht, I wad dee" which was included in Alan Ramsay's *Tea-Table Miscellany*, 1724. It tells of youthful love blighted by the envy and greedy materialism of the young man's family but its assertion of a stoical cheerfulness concealing a deeper sadness must have had a special appeal for its writer. For Grisell Baillie was also a heroine of a quite remarkably selfless, cheerful and stoical kind. "She was", writes her daughter, Lady Murray of Stan-hope, "the eldest of eighteen children my grandmother bore, except two, that died infants".[2] Her father, Sir Patrick Home, was a noted Covenanter and the whole family endured anti-Presbyterian persecution during the troubles of Charles II's reign. When Grisell Home was only twelve years old, she was sent by her father from their country-house to Edinburgh, a long journey, when my grandfather Baillie was first imprisoned, (my grandfathers being early and intimate friends, connected by the same way of thinking in religion and politics), to try if, by her age, she could get admittance into the prison unsuspected, and slip a letter into his hand, of advice and information, and bring back what intelligence she could. She succeeded so well in both, that from that time I reckon her hardships began, from the confidence that was put in her and the activity she naturally had far beyond her age, in executing whatever she was intrusted with.[3]

On one later occasion before the exile of the family in Utrecht, Sir Patrick hid for a month in a vault under ground at Polwarth Church a mile from the family house. Here is Lady Murray's description of her mother's succour of her father, Sir Patrick:

She went every night by herself at midnight, to carry him victuals and drink, and stayed with him as long as she could to get home before day. . . . She at that time had a terror for a church-yard, especially in the dark as is not uncommon at her age, by idle nursery stories; but when engaged by concern for her father, she stumbled over the graves every night alone without fear of any kind entering her thoughts, but for soldiers, and parties in search of him, which the least noise or motion of a leaf put her in terror for.[4]

While Sir Patrick was so concealed he had no light beyond an open slit at one end of the vault and his comfort and entertainment was to repeat to himself the Latin Psalms of George Buchanan which he had by heart. Here is his granddaughter again:

Two years before he died which was in 1724 [Lady Grisell would then be 59], I was witness to his desiring my mother to take up that book, which amongst others always lay upon his table, and bid her try if he had forgot his Psalms, by naming any one she would have him repeat; and by casting her eye over it, she would know if he was right, though she did not understand it; and he missed not a word in any place she named to him, and said, they had been the great comfort of his life, by night and day, on all occasions.[5]

Sir Patrick Home was an old man by then and there can be no question about the mutual love and regard of father and daughter but there is, nevertheless, something oddly displaced about his praise of the Psalms to the daughter who still cannot read them and who surely herself would have been more properly described as the great comfort of his life. Lady Grisell Baillie cheerfully sacrificed her literary concerns on the altar of domestic piety. As the eldest child in this large family she acted throughout the period of exile in Utrecht as little mother. Her daughter's description of her intellectual and writing life may stand as a monument to all the other women after her who put love and care before the more selfish activity of writing.

> My mother when she had a moment's time, took a lesson with the rest in French and Dutch, and also diverted herself with music. I have now a book of songs of her writing when there; many of them interrupted, half writ, some broke off in the middle of a sentence.[6]

Her celebrated song tends to appeal to modern taste because of its narrative disruptions: it begins in youthful hope and ends in ageing sorrow but in between it is organized emotionally rather than chronologically; its art is peculiarly mimetic of its creator's life. And it is a confirmation of Lady Grisell Baillie's female selflessness that it reserves its deepest sympathy for the disappointed male lover:

> His bonnet stood aye fu' round on his brow;
> His auld ane look'd better than mony ane's new;
> But now he lets 't wear ony gait it will hing,
> And casts himsel' dowie upon the corn-bing.

And now he gaes daundrin' about the dykes,
And a' he dow do is to hound the tykes:
The live-lang nicht he ne'er steeks his e'e;
And werena my heart licht I wad dee.[7]

It is the final, although admirable, irony of Lady Grisell Baillie's life that her largest and most coherent literary monument should be her *Household Book*. Every careful entry in the book speaks the woman, yet none actually sanctions self-revelation.[8]

When Joanna Baillie, possibly a descendant of Lady Grisell Baillie, came to write Lady Grisell's story in one of her *Metrical Legends*, 1821, it is the heroine and not the writer that she celebrates. Joanna Baillie rather ominously remarks in her Preface to the *Legends* that women are privileged to be able to be unlearned:

> Women have this desirable privilege over the other sex, that they may be unlearned without any implied inferiority; and I hope our modern zeal for education will never proceed far enough to deprive them of this great advantage. At the same time they may avowedly and creditably possess as much learning, either in science or languages as they can fairly and honestly attain, the neglect of more necessary occupations being here considered as approaching to a real breach of rectitude.[9]

Accordingly she uses the example of Lady Grisell to reprove literary women, bluestockings who neglect household cares.

> Or she, whose cultured, high-strained talents soar
> Through all th'ambitious range of letter'd lore
> With soul enthusiastic, fondly smitten
> With all that e'er in classic page was written,
> And whilst her wit in critic task engages,
> The echoed praise of all praised things outrages;
> Whose finger, white and small, with ink-stain tipt,
> Still scorns with vulgar thimble to be clipt;
> Who doth with proud pretence her claims advance
> To philosophic, honour'd ignorance

Of all, that, in divided occupation,
Gives the base stamp of female degradation;

. . .

Will she, I trow, or any kirtled sage,
Admire the subject of my artless page?[10]

Joanna Baillie was nearly sixty when she published her *Metrical Legends* and she had always been conservative in feeling. But the contrast between the reproof of ink-stained ladies and the extensive pennings of the reprover indicates her insecurity about her own activity – to write is bad enough but to cry up one's writing is unthinkable.

Not many eighteenth-century women writers had Lady Grisell Baillie's excuses of pressing domesticity but most of them shared her self-effacement to the extent indeed of a seriously crippling female self-deprecation about the written word. Alison Cockburn (*née* Rutherford) (1713–94) and Jean Elliot (1727–1805) provided the two equally well known versions of "The Flowers of the Forest". They were both renowned for their wit and resourcefulness, yet they were both unwilling to admit authorship of the songs that have made them famous. Yet these are in different ways songs of female experience, for although they are probably laments for the dead in battle, it is bereft women who are the real subjects of the poems, particularly of Jean Elliot's version:

At e'en in the gloaming, nae younkers are roaming,
   'Bout stacks, with the lasses at bogle to play;
But ilk maid sits dreary, lamenting her deary –
   The flowers of the forest are weded awae.[11]

Alison Cockburn moved in Edinburgh literary circles, corresponded with Hume, Monboddo and Burns, but stated in 1775, "I am very certain that no woman ought to write anything but from the heart to the heart; never for the public eye, without male correction", and later, "As for printing, never fear. I hate print".[12] Jean Elliot who also socialized freely and had a reputation as an anecdotalist, responded to a request from Somerville on behalf of Sir Walter Scott for an "exact copy" of her version by complying but asking that her name "may not be mentioned" – Scott thought her effacement "somewhat prudish".[13]

Lady Anne Lindsay Barnard is known to us primarily for her song "Auld Robin Gray" the authorship of which she only admitted late and under pressure. She too was reputed to be a wit and accomplished story-teller:

> She was entertaining a large party of distinguished guests at dinner when a hitch occurred in the kitchen. Her old servant came up behind her, and said, "My Lady, you must tell another story – the second course won't be ready for five minutes".[14]

She wrote intelligent letters from the Cape Province where her husband was Secretary, to her family, to Henry Melville, Viscount Dundas, then Secretary for War, and to Lord Macartney after his retiral as Governor of the Cape, but none of these was published until after her death and there remain interdictions on many of her papers. Indeed the whole notion of writing things down to serve as reminders for subsequent writing provoked in her a sense of shame which she admittedly calls false but nevertheless does not overcome:

> I often wish, when I hear anything new, curious, or useful, that I could divest myself of that portion of false shame which prevents me from taking out a memorandum-book and marking it down while I remember the particulars, which afterwards escape my memory, and the thing sinks into oblivion. But for a woman very ill-informed on most subjects – I might have said on *all* subjects – to give herself the *air* of wisdom, while she knows how superficial she is, by marking down anything that passes in company, I cannot endure it! It is wilfully drawing on a pair of blue stockings she has no right to wear! In this I often put myself in mind of what an old friend used to say to us when children at her feasts: "My dears, eat as much as you *can*, but pocket nothing". Was I a man, I would pocket without shame. It becomes at some time or another useful to him, and teaches the mind the good habit of reflecting on what it hears.[15]

For these women being an avowed writer partakes of self-display, involves indecorousness at least. Publication is an aggressive act and those writers who do descend to the market-place have to find more powerful motives for doing so than self-promotion. And so Joanna Baillie and Mary Brunton and Susan Ferrier would have it that they are doing us good by showing us how to behave. Now, of course, the didactic claim is not confined to women; it is commonplace in the justification of the novel and drama in the eighteenth and early nineteenth centuries to claim an educative function, even in cases like the notorious *Les Liaisons Dangereuses* where the effect seems to be quite at odds with the expressed intention. Didacticism is, of course, aggressive in itself but it is the aggression of the wise parent who must be firm to be kind rather than the aggression of the *enfant terrible* who must be self-displaying to be free. And these Scottish women writers, all of them unhypocritically religious, seem to have had an unusually unaffected conviction about the improving nature of their work.

Even so none of them courted publicity, although all of them sought publication. The first volume of Joanna Baillie's series of verse dramas was widely assumed to be by a man and her authorship was not acknowledged until 1800, two years after its publication. Susan Ferrier clung to anonymity despite being, like her eighteenth-century predecessors, a lively conversationalist – to be a social asset was felt to be properly feminine, to court the publicity of print, even to make readers better, was another matter. Scott praised Susan Ferrier's social talents in particular:

> Miss Ferrier . . . besides having great talents has conversation the least *exigeante* of any author, female at least, whom I have ever seen among the long list I have encountered, – simple, full of humour, and exceedingly ready at repartee; and all this without the least affectation of the blue stocking.[16]

Men and women alike were anxious to avoid the imputation of bluestockingdom – our contemporary equivalent is probably the equally suspect denials of being a feminist that one tends to hear.

In terms of women's work Mary Brunton is the most interesting of the three: she was not prolific like Joanna Baillie, or as funny and versatile in the depiction of contemporary manners as Susan Ferrier but, apart from herself having a typically female death in childbirth, she did think about what it might be like for a woman to make her living without resorting to governessing. She does not put a pen in the hand of Laura, the heroine of her first novel, *Self-Control*, 1810 – we have to wait for Catherine Carswell to do that – but she does put a pencil there. Laura's good but weak father has been endeavouring ineffectually to provide for his daughter's future which he has already jeopardized by financial incompetence; he is not even aware of the extent of his poverty and Laura, rejecting the female way of marriage for money (her admirer is a rake, a more unpleasant version of Clarissa's Lovelace) tries to sell her talented pictures. Her efforts with three London dealers meet with misunderstanding or insult in a way that clearly shows Laura's position as representative. A painting from later in the century by Emily Mary Osborn, *Nameless and Friendless*, 1857, probably depicts a similar situation: it was certainly taken to do so by the *Art Journal* in 1864.[17] Both Brunton and Osborn seem then to be investigating the possibility of women becoming professional in the arts. But both seem to me to be not merely suggesting that women attempting to earn their living should not be met with contumely, but also half acquiescing, however paradoxical this might seem, in the feeling that women should not be forced to earn their living. Emily Osborn's painting depicts her young woman standing with modestly downcast eyes while a supercilious older man appraises her picture and two fashionable younger men appraise her. Beside her, holding a portfolio, is a boy, perhaps her brother, who is looking aggressively at the dealer: by implication the pale, pretty young woman is in need of a protector more manly than the lad can be. In *Self-Control* Laura's picture is bought by her admirer and eventual husband, De Courcy, who also commissions a companion piece, while swearing the dealer to secrecy about his identity. De Courcy admires Laura for being above the vulgar prejudice against women being useful but, nevertheless, there is no suggestion that Laura continues to paint as anything other than a recreation after she has married for love and secured a competence upon which to live.

It is to Mrs Oliphant that we must turn for the first really professional Scottish woman writer who neither denigrated her profession nor represented work as undesirable for other women, although none of her working women is a professional writer.[18] Mrs Oliphant's work is too well known to need much further remark but I do want to stress the continuing relationship between the domestic sphere and the activity of writing even though the emphasis has subtly shifted. It is common knowledge that Margaret Oliphant wore a hole in her finger writing to support her extended family, among other things to send her sons to Eton. Lady Grisell Baillie could hardly start writing because of her domestic responsibilities, Margaret Oliphant could hardly stop because of hers. Here she is in her *Autobiography* describing an averted financial crisis: there is no money, her latest novel has been refused, she goes home in despair to a house that is cheerful and comfortable but in which no one is able to share her responsibilities:

> No one thought anything more than that I was dull or cross for the rest of the evening. I used to work very late then, always till two in the morning (it is past three at this moment, 18th, nay, 19th April 1895, but this is no longer usual with me). I can't remember whether I worked that night, but I think it was one of the darkest nights (oh, no, no, that I should say so! they were all safe and well), at least a very dreadful moment, and I could not think what I should do.[19]

In the morning a man came from the *Graphic* to ask for a story, eventually offering £1300. "Our Father in heaven had settled it all the time for the children; there had never been any doubt. I was absolutely without hope or help. I did not know where to turn, and here, in a moment, all was clear again – the road free in the sunshine, the cloud in a moment rolled away."[20]

It is Mrs Oliphant's great triumph and great tragedy that her memorial should be her work and not her family: all her children predeceased her, nor indeed did her sons achieve anything very much in their lives. Her *Autobiography* concludes with words that I cannot reread without tears:

> In the last four years after Cyril was taken from us, we were nearer and nearer. I can hear myself saying "Cecco and I." It was the constant phrase. But all through he was getting weaker; and I knew it, and tried not to know.
> And now here I am all alone.
> I cannot write any more.[21]

It is easier, however, to make money from fiction and journalism than from poetry – it is unlikely that Mrs Oliphant would have got her sons to Eton had her talent been for verse. Janet Hamilton (1795–1873) was married at thirteen and brought up a large family; her experience in Lanarkshire mining communities places decency among the highest virtues in her pantheon and she does not hesitate to satirize the women who fail to achieve it:

> 'Bout the wives in oor location,
> An' the lasses' botheration,
> Some are decent, some are dandies,
> An' a gey wheen drucken randies,
> Aye to neebors' hooses sailin',
> Greetin' bairns ahint them trailin',
> Gaun for nouther bread nor butter,
> Jist to drink an' rin the cutter.
> Oh, the dreadfu' curse o' drinkin'!
> Men are ill, but tae my thinkin',
> Leukin' through the drucken fock,
> There's a Jenny for ilk Jock.[22]

Increasingly among the women writers of the respectable working and lower middle classes the female struggle and the class struggle merge. Two Glasgow poets, Marion Bernstein, an invalided music teacher, and Jessie Russell, a dressmaker before her marriage, write fiercely of the oppression of working-class women. Tom Leonard includes in his collection *Radical Renfrew*[23] poems by both women. Marion Bernstein's "A Rule to Work Both Ways" is particularly savage:

If beating can reform a wife
  It might reform a husband too,
Since such are the effects of strife –
  My sisters, I advise that you

Should try it, not with fists – Oh, no!
  For that would seem like some weak joker;
In husband-curing let each blow
  Be given with the kitchen poker![24]

Tom Leonard is obviously right to anthologize the poems he does but a look through *Mirren's Musings*, Marion Bernstein's collection of poems, shows that her whole outlook is a little compromised by rather facile piety and coyly pawky wit and Jessie Russell's radicalism is conveyed by either lame or banally conventional verse. In spite, therefore, of this poetic radicalism, the truly subversive possibilities of women's writing in itself have still to be fully explored. And this brings me to my last two women – Catherine Carswell and Willa Muir.

In her best known work, *Open the Door!*, 1920, Catherine Carswell, like Mary Brunton, displaces her heroine Joanna's professional commitment into the visual arts but, unlike Mary Brunton, she shows the work important for itself. In the less well esteemed *The Camomile*, 1922, the woman writer as heroine emerges. Ellen Carstairs has no time for the conventional pieties of domesticity: she wonders what her friend Laura would think if she knew that her marriage had been the motive force for one of Ellen's short stories: "She would say that I had no right to use any such knowledge as material for fiction, all such knowledge being 'sacred'. Oh, that word! Are not the uses of art more sacred than a million domesticities?"[25] She herself rejects a conventional marriage to an upstanding young doctor; she recognizes that in order to retain conventional middle-class life as subject matter, it may be necessary to detach herself from it:

"I know at last to what world I irrevocably belong, and that it is not Duncan's world. I have found this out in time. And because of it I have the whole of Duncan's world to write about. One can never write till one stands outside."[26]

But it may not be possible for a woman to stand outside every area of experience. In the autobiography which she left unfinished at her death, Catherine Carswell speculates about potentially taboo areas for women writers. She explains that she had been reading a volume of verse by a woman which contained the record of an unhappy love affair. The poem induced in her a feeling of discomfort as at impropriety which she cannot explain away by saying that the execution was inadequate:

> Do we . . . feel perfectly comfortable when we read the love poems of the Brontës, or Christina Rossetti, or Mrs Browning, or the love confessions of a Marie Bashkirtseff, the married confessions of a Sophie Tolstoi? . . .
>
> To begin with the question seems a simple one. Is a woman writer fundamentally handicapped in a whole important sphere of verbal expression? If so, why? It was agreed that this looked like the real snag. The man can give himself (and others) away passionately, wittily, blatantly, imperfectly, coarsely, neurotically, without the reader feeling that his effort or his achievement was unsuitable to a man. Without liking or commending the autobiographer's character one can read and judge of what he wrote: Rousseau can say anything: so can George Moore: so can Keats in his letters, and a thousand others, English or not English, without offending any reader save on moral grounds; and morality here does not enter, because be the woman never so moral, she can still offend by the mere intimacy of her confession. Is there a marked, an essential disparity between men and women? The woman because she is a woman, must as an artist suppress what the man as artist or as man is entitled to reveal.[27]

The debate here is more firmly entering theoretical realms. The battle for the right to write, the struggle for the material conditions that will make women's writing possible has hugely advanced since Lady Grisell Baillie laid down her pen and put on her thimble but the constrictions of a possibly socially constructed gender are less easily defined and hence less easily combatted. Vast quantities of feminist theory have rolled through the presses since Willa Muir wrote *Women: An Inquiry* in 1925 but the issues that she defined then remain to tease us today.

Willa Muir seeks to discover if there is any essential difference between men and women – "An essential difference would be a difference distinctively human, that is spiritual as well as physical, and at the same time distinctively sexual"[28] – and hence if the creative work of women is different in kind from the creative work of men. She concludes the definition of her aims by observing that the

> subordination of women makes it difficult but not impossible to recognise the essential quality of womanhood. In a masculine civilisation the creative work of women may be belittled, misinterpreted, or denied: but if it is a reality, its existence will be proved at least by the emotional colour of the denial.[29]

Like many of her successors in this inquiry Willa Muir is better at defining the problems and asking the questions than she is at providing the answers, but as theoretical underpinning, her essay remains a significant landmark.

Willa Muir's arguments include many points that have now become very familiar and may, because we have had more time to see the pitfalls which surround them, arouse our opposition. She remarks women's potential for creating human beings and men's for creating abstract systems, she finds women more in touch with the unconscious and men with conscious life, she credits women with intuitive and men with rational perceptions, she sets women's creative love against men's creative thought. In short she works with some of the binary oppositions that we have come rather to distrust. But in no sense does she countenance the use of such distinctions to curtail women's potential. "Men", she comments tartly, "can prove their theories even when they are wrong; women cannot prove their intuitions even when they are right.

In his world, that of organized form, man dominates women naturally".[30] She goes on to dissolve her own oppositions and to produce a version of the androgynous artist which is still attractive as a theoretical option. "The artist must thus possess both masculine and feminine qualities; that is to say, he has immediate access to the intuitions of unconscious life, as a woman has, and he creates conscious form as a man does".[31] Historically, however, she finds that women have excelled in literature among the arts and in the novel within literature. She concludes:

> the conception of womanhood which has been adumbrated here, if it is accepted, demands . . . many adjustments in the attitude of women towards themselves, towards morality, religion, sex, and education . . . it is impossible within the limits of this essay to give even a hint of them.[32]

The process of adjustment continues.

Debateable Land:
The Prose Work of Violet Jacob

Carol Anderson

Violet Jacob (1863–1946) is probably a name unfamiliar to many readers. Those who have heard of her are likely to be Scots, and even they may have a somewhat vague impression of her work, gained from browsing in anthologies of Scottish poetry. Jacob is generally known as a poet who wrote primarily in Scots in the early twentieth century, her poetry dealing mainly with rural life in Angus. She has been seen on the whole as a minor regional poet, sometimes as a rather sentimental one; one critic even dubbed her "shrinking Violet".[1] It is a pity that Violet Jacob has had so faint and floral a reputation, because, like countless women writers who have been long overlooked – and there are many in Scotland – she is a writer of much greater interest than is usually supposed, altogether more vigorous and "modern". It is heartening to note that there are now signs of interest in her work, for she certainly deserves reassessment.[2]

For a start, her work is much wider in range than is usually realized. Besides poetry in Scots and English, she wrote fiction, mostly historical novels and romances, several of which are very fine, notably *Flemington* (1911), a novel set in eighteenth-century Scotland and a powerful work worthy of much wider recognition. Jacob also published several volumes of short stories, books for children and a family history, the last mentioned more interesting than it may sound, for

Jacob, before her marriage a Kennedy-Erskine, belonged to an ancient family with an estate at Dun in Angus, and a long and colourful past. Diaries and letters she wrote during years she spent in India with her army officer husband came to light in the 1980s and are now in print.[3] Besides her literary work, Violet Jacob was also a skilled artist, illustrating children's books on which she collaborated with friends, and painting scenes from the world around her, especially in India. Her paintings of Indian flora are especially accomplished and are held by the Royal Botanical Gardens in Edinburgh.

She was well regarded in her own time, received an Honorary degree (an LL.D.) from Edinburgh University in 1936, and had a number of "literary" friendships with writers such as John Buchan, who greatly admired her, and A.E. Housman, who was for a time a neighbour. Yet today her work is largely out of print, and until recently was barely mentioned in literary histories, far less critical studies of Scottish literature. In "English" literature she is probably unknown.

There are, perhaps, several obstacles to appreciation of her work. Her very diversity, like that of writers such as Naomi Mitchison and Margaret Oliphant, may count against her in the "seriousness" stakes. Then, too, there is the question of the forms in which she wrote, which are almost all of uncertain literary status. However, a deeper understanding of both why she is so neglected and why she is so interesting, may be gained by taking a broad view of her cultural circumstances, and her response to them. Violet Jacob has been undervalued, I believe, for reasons which relate both to her Scottishness and to her femaleness.

This can be seen if we look at Hugh MacDiarmid's assessment of her. Certainly he did consider her, in 1925, as "by far the most considerable of contemporary vernacular poets"[4], while her prose work he judged "respectable". He had no time, however, for her short stories, and on the whole his praise is faint, his tone patronizing. He had, ultimately, one major, overriding objection to Violet Jacob. She did not, he believed, engage with the problems of Scotland's political situation which so exercised him. Now, it is true that if we read her letters and diaries from India, she sometimes refers to

England and the English when she might more accurately have talked of Britain and the British. This is all the more frustrating when we know she had a Scottish father and upbringing, was writing to her Welsh mother, and had an Irish husband. But this is not what bothers MacDiarmid, who never read her letters and diaries. He complains, rather, about her fiction; what irks MacDiarmid is that although her imagination was stirred by Scotland, she doesn't *assert* Scottishness. Her Scottishness is a "quality of her being", he says. "She cannot descend to argument, even within herself" (p. 8). He snarls about "the divided, and in the last analysis, ineffectual nature of her prose work" (p. 9), and "her apparent obliviousness to the vital problems confronting Scottish nationality today, which a better-oriented spirit with her raciality of character could not have refrained from addressing" (p. 10). MacDiarmid's invective highlights the difficulties facing both Scottish writers and critics. Since the Union with England, Scottish culture has maintained a sense of separate identity, and yet been weakened and plagued by insecurity; it is arguably a case of the "colonial mentality". MacDiarmid set himself up to combat this, but his aggressive stance and proscriptive approach could be damaging as well as invigorating.

Undoubtedly Violet Jacob's work has limitations; some of her poetry is nostalgic in a typically Scottish way for which there are historical reasons. But MacDiarmid's approach does not acknowledge her strengths, or address certain important questions. Indeed, even her way of expressing Scottishness as it were unconsciously could be seen more positively, not as a weakness, but as a condition worth aspiring to – the assumption that one's subject matter has significance. The issue of "Scottishness" may cloud perception of the work itself. It is worth remarking, too (a point ignored by most critics), that she was fascinated not only by Scotland, but also by Wales and the Welsh borderlands, unsurprisingly since she had a Welsh mother and lived for some time with her husband in the Welsh Marches. This interest in some ways parallels her Scottish interests. However, I think Violet Jacob's work, her prose work in particular, is at times, in fact, much more radical and questioning than MacDiarmid recognizes, although not necessarily along the lines he would have liked.

In some of her short stories especially – and among these I see excellence where MacDiarmid sees none – she engages with issues of power and identity, often as part of a general preoccupation with Scottish culture which pervades her work.

More specifically, some of what I see as Violet Jacob's most interesting (and radical) fiction deals with the experience of women in Scottish society. This is not her only, or even her central concern, perhaps, but in her handling of such themes in her neglected short stories particularly, Jacob becomes a writer really to reckon with. MacDiarmid, with his masculine concept of Scottishness (the one that has prevailed) appears blind to this aspect of her work, and probably it would not in any case have been congenial to him; Jacob has been underestimated in part because she was a woman, and a writer with particular kinds of interest.

Several of Violet Jacob's most interesting stories are contained in a collection called *Tales of My Own Country*, published in 1922, and unfortunately out of print. The title is worth remarking in a writer whose use of language was always precise. Here Violet Jacob lays imaginative claim to her territory: the "country" could be Scotland, of course; more specifically it is the "country" of Angus, where Violet Jacob grew up and which she deeply loved. The stories set out to map and give literary life to the area and its people, each story being economically told but rich in detail, evoking the spirit of place, while, as a perceptive French critic observed, the landscape serves to heighten our perception of the principal characters.[5] The lives in these stories, like those in Joyce's *Dubliners*, are mainly frustrated and obscure, the characters mostly solitaries, outsiders, eccentrics, generally poor and often female; but in the best of these stories the quality of the writing gives them significance. This volume is perhaps an assertion of imaginative power from the "margins".

A good illustration of Violet Jacob's interests can be found in one story, "The Debatable Land", not necessarily her most substantial, but brilliantly focused, and in some ways emblematic of her work more generally. Again it is worth taking special note of the story's title. Dictionary definitions of "debateable ground" (Scots usage keeps the middle "e", though the story was published without it) suggest such ideas as "ground, literally or figuratively, over which there is contention; borderland". It is also significant that "debateable land" was traditionally known to be that on the border between England and Scotland (in the area of Liddesdale), with all the cultural and political connotations that implies. The image of borderland is symbolically apt in other ways, too, for Violet Jacob's work often engages with questions of moral ambiguity, the "borderlands" of judgement. The idea of divided loyalty, explored by other Scottish writers such as Scott and Stevenson, is central to her novel *Flemington*, with its Jacobite–Hanoverian theme, in which the figure of the double agent is important. Violet Jacob's own work, although it raises questions of moral judgement, is singularly "unjudging" in character, inviting debate rather than asserting answers.

In the story "The Debatable Land", some of these themes and ideas come together; as the volume and the story are out of print, I will briefly outline the plot. The central character is Jessie Mary, an orphan who, on the death of her grandmother, is hired out as a servant to Mrs Muirhead, a cottager in the parish. Mrs Muirhead's son, Peter, imagines he can make a sexual conquest of Jessie Mary, and troubles her so much that on one occasion she takes refuge with a gypsy man camping on the nearby piece of "debateable land", which belongs to no one. Soon after this, the Muirheads' black hen goes missing, and Peter suspects the gypsy. Before Peter can tell the police, Jessie Mary goes down to the gypsy's tent by night to warn him. At the end we see the two – Jessie Mary and the gypsy – slip away together in the dawn light. The story ends: "And, in the debatable land among the brambles, a few black feathers blew on the morning wind."[6]

The story is as economically told as anything by Katherine Mansfield, charting the young woman's movement from captivity to a dubious liberty. We see Jessie Mary trapped in her life with her employers; the yard of the cottage where she works "contained a row of hen-coops and a sty enclosing a pig whose proportions waxed as autumn waned" (p. 68). In this one sentence there are three images of enclosure: the yard itself, the hen-coops and the sty. Jessie Mary, it is implied, is trapped like the animals, and even her employers themselves are not free, for their land, in turn, belongs to the laird, who rides by to inspect his property. Jessie Mary is shown trapped by lack of money and property; she is also a woman. She herself is tough and unconventional, having grown up, we are told, in relative freedom: "She was a fierce-looking lass with her hot grey eyes" (p. 68). Ironically, her very freedom from artifice is what incites Peter: "The girl was looking at him with eyes whose directness a youth of his type is liable to misunderstand" (p. 69). Her sexual oppressor is, of course, in a position of peculiar power as her employer's son.

Here, as elsewhere in her work, Violet Jacob presents the workings of sexual power and conflict. Jessie Mary rejects Peter's unwanted attentions in a passage of surprising violence:

> She had felt his hot breath in her ear, and, in her fury, pushed him from her with such violence that he staggered back against a weak place in the yard fence and fell through, cutting his elbow on a piece of broken glass. She stood staring at him, half terrified at what she had done, but rejoicing to see the blood trickle down his sleeve. She would have liked to kill him. (p. 73)

And this is the work of "Shrinking Violet"! Characteristically, though, Jacob underscores the theme of sexual oppression through a comic motif, lightening the tone with the image of the trapped, fussy hens like "vindictive dowagers", a parody of conventional femininity, with their master, "the Dorking cock, self-conscious and gallant" (p. 72), an ironic contrast with the ungallant Peter.

The text also suggests more explicitly the powerlessness of the central female character:

> Life for her had always been a sort of inevitable accident, a state in whose ordering she had no part as a whole, however much choice she might have had in its details. But now there was little choice [even] in these . . . . (p. 72)

The debateable land, the free land belonging to no one, described in its autumn colours as a place of wild and luxuriant natural beauty, is the place where Jessie Mary looks and feels most at home. Thus when she rejects the claims of others and attempts to take control of her own life, it is symbolically apt that she flees into the debateable land, and indeed that the black hen (suggestive of domestic confinement) is stolen, and possibly eaten. Another, specifically Scots sense of "debateable" comes into play here: the sense of "able to shift for one's self; energetic".

Jacob's work is subtle, rarely providing straightforward "happy endings". Jessie Mary's flight with the gypsy is not, perhaps, unequivocally a flight to freedom. The cool, impersonal ending is ambiguous: "Day broke on the figures of a man and woman who descended the slope of the fields towards the road. The man walked first" (p. 86). This is at first sight maybe a slight, if well made, short fiction, but I think that the almost cinematic conclusion contributes to an effect that justifies comparison with the work of Thomas Hardy;[7] Jacob's French critic also compared her with Guy de Maupassant.

Other comparisons could usefully be made; this and other works by Violet Jacob might be placed in the Scottish literary tradition to the enrichment of both. In her imagery of land, of landed and landless people, the aristocratic Violet Jacob might be compared to Walter Scott, whose influence can be seen in her novels. The comparison, however, emphasizes her more radical Romanticism. Scott, as F.R. Hart points out, "confessed to an embarrassing affection for the rootless or duplicitous people who belong to borderlands, debateable lands: smugglers, reivers, pirates, gipsies".[8] But despite Scott's fondness for the vagabonds of his fiction, who often express the spirit of Scottish culture, there is in his work, an underlying emphasis on the need for a stable structure in society, and this is related to the idea and actuality of property. As Alexander Welsh says, "Property exerts and responds to a workable order in society and keeps individual passions in check"; it is "the right to things as presently constituted: realty is practically the same thing as reality".[9] Violet Jacob is fascinated by vagrant figures, by borderlands, physical, symbolic and moral, and although her prose is always controlled, there is in her work a deeper underlying sympathy for the lawless and the

disinherited than Scott ever allows himself fully to acknowledge.

At her best, Violet Jacob is capable of exposing and
exploring deep and powerful emotions, especially through
"marginalized" figures, as can be seen in another remarkable
story called "Thievie", brought back into print quite
recently.[10] In this story, the central character is again a
woman, Janet Robb, thirty-four years old, and like Jessie
Mary, unselfconscious and strong-willed. She is described as
"a thickset, bony woman, one of those who, unremarkable in
feature, are yet remarkable in presence, and though in daily
life she made no bid for attractiveness, it was because she did
not happen to know where, as in what, attraction lay" (p. 4).
She has so far lived out her life in caring for her miserly old
father, and when she realizes that he is in danger of drowning
in a local flood, she is tempted to leave him to his fate.
But, fearing he will take with him his carefully hoarded little
fortune, she sets out to save him, with thoughts of her own
future. She has recently met a man who is interested in her,
but her marriage would depend on her inheritance. Loss of
that means to her loss of much more. She reaches her father
and rescues him; but he suspects her motive, and in their
battle of wills, he falls into the river and drowns, taking his
money with him rather than let her have any.

It is remarkably strong stuff when we consider that,
according to one commentary, Jacob's stories "seldom rise
above the level of rural sentimentality".[11] It is, in fact, a tale
of parricide in spirit if not in deed, in which the mounting
waters of the flood symbolically parallel the rising anger of
the woman. The reader is granted access to Janet's thoughts
when she is suddenly kissed by Willie Black, who points out
to her that she is a slave to her father; she thinks of all her
years of work on the ferry with her father, and the lack of love
between them:

> She had no fear of work and had taken it as a normal
> condition, but it had come between herself and all that
> was worth having; the toil that had been a man's toil,
> not a woman's, had built a barrier round her to cut her
> off from a woman's life. All this had lurked, unrecognised

in her mind, but now it had leaped up, aroused by a man's careless, familiar horseplay.

Her breath came quick as she thought of her own meagre stake in the world. She knew herself for some kind of a power, and that was awaking the dormant realisation of her slavery, all the more bitter for its long sleep. (p. 16)

The passage is all the more complex in its implications when we realize that Willie Black, who taunts her, is no more than a fortune-hunter, and indeed Janet herself is not a fully sympathetic figure; she is described as having inherited "her father's love of money-making" (p. 13). Yet Janet's aspirations to conventionality – "She had a queer longing to be like other women, a factor in the male world" (p. 13) – are shown to be an outcome of her powerlessness. The only route to power in a society in which women are economically dependent, is through gaining male approval. An apparently minor detail is further revealing: the small fortune amassed by Davie Robb, "Thievie", is substantially made up of money sent by "a son who had left home early and was making a good income in Canada" (p. 8). Thus Janet is not only dependent on the world of men, but on wealth created outside Scotland, in the colonies. The story illustrates, in its compressed way, how the different aspects of Janet's frustration – economic, sexual, psychological, emotional – are interrelated. This is one reason why the end of the story is, I think, genuinely touching. When Janet is brought ashore, without father, without fortune, without future, one of the men from the village:

took off his coat and wrapped it round her. She seemed oblivious of his action. "Hae", said he, with clumsy kindness, "pit it on, lass. What'll yer lad say gin ye starve?"
Janet thrust the coat from her. (p. 36)

This is characteristic Jacob prose: understated, but resonant with meaning.

Equally interesting for its portrayal of a woman caught in power structures, although in this case unaware of them, is her little-discussed novella *The Lum Hat*, also made available in print in recent years.[12] The central character is a young woman, Christina Mills, who has never left her home in a small Scottish coastal town. The title alludes to the tall black chimney-pot hat worn by her banker father; the hat, we are told "was as much part of the community as the wooden Highlander who had stood for some generations at a tobacconist's door in the Seagate, or the spire of the parish kirk" (p. 3). The image of the tall black hat "like a third presence" (p. 3) in the church when Christina and her father are sitting there, is deeply suggestive, hinting at the repressive forces at work in the community and in the woman's subjectivity: the role of the father, of convention and of religion. When a possible suitor, a worldly sea captain called Baird, comes wooing the inexperienced Christina, we are told:

> To avoid setting her eyes on Baird as he came through the church door, she looked upwards at the great mass of stonework towering pointed above them to its weather vane and received from the moving clouds beyond it the sensation of being under something that was falling on her. (p. 9)

Such a passage suggests matters that are delicately explored as the text unfolds. The latent powers of imagination and sexuality are implied. Christina encounters a gypsy woman selling brooms, who urges her "'Ye should get a man . . . . Get you a man that'll tak' ye awa and gie ye a sicht of the world'" (p. 7), and this woman becomes associated in her mind with Baird: "She was faintly uncomfortable in their presence. They touched some sleeping thing in her mind which feared to be awakened" (p. 10). Christina is unable to break from the ways and influences of her family and early life, even when an opportunity for a "fuller experience" presents itself.

The stories touched on here illustrate Jacob's remarkably "modern" engagement with issues of gender and power, but it would be unfair to leave the impression that her work is peopled only with bitter or repressed characters. There is loss and disappointment in her fiction, but also a dry humour, and at times the comic spirit prevails. The handling of her female characters is complex in perspective, and while male characters are sometimes brutal or weak, they are also at times sympathetically explored, as in the novel *Flemington*, for instance. Traditional gender roles are frequently interrogated, in various ways. Another story in *Tales of My Own Country*, "The Figurehead", deals with a young man's inability to reconcile the ideal, as embodied for him in the ship's figurehead, and the actual woman with whom he has an affair on shore. Jacob's fiction returns to some of the same ideas and preoccupations, but from different angles.

The idea of Violet Jacob as a limited writer is further challenged by the existence of her Indian writings. These offer another perspective on a writer whose scope has been underestimated; at the same time, they raise some larger questions. The extent and complexity of Scottish writing in relation to Empire and to colonialism has not yet been fully explored, and the case of someone like Violet Jacob is complicated and interesting. Many Scots benefited from the Empire, some directly, others more indirectly; yet, as some critics have suggested, the Scots' relationship to Empire may be subtly different from that of the English, being in some ways that of colonized turned colonizers.

The letters and diaries Violet Jacob wrote during her years in India illustrate the complexity of her experience and her ambivalence, showing that she was deeply attracted to Indian culture, and yet also deeply responsive to a sense of Otherness, which sometimes appalled her. She also felt herself in some ways detached from the British society she encountered in India under the Raj, although she had friends among the colonial community there. It is interesting to speculate how far as a woman and a Scot, and one of aristocratic birth, she was both inside and outside the colonial Establishment. It is also interesting to speculate how far her concern with outsider figures in her fiction is related to her own experience of living on the "borders" of both Indian and British expatriate society, as well, perhaps as the experience of being a woman artist moving in "society" circles and yet deeply attached to the farm folk of Angus.

Obviously, I am merely touching on a vast area of ideas here, and have not room to do more than glance at Violet

Jacob's "colonial" writings in the form of one short story from a collection called *The Fortune Hunters*, most of which are pot-boilers and not her best. One story, "The Fringe of the Jungle", is more interesting than the others.[13] It deals, although less deeply, with a theme similar to that of Conrad's *Heart of Darkness*, concerning itself with a European man in India who becomes temporarily mad, apparently possessed by the soul of a dead Indian murderer. The story could easily seem to exemplify European fears of the supposed savagery of India. However, the framing devices of the narrative, the use of a tale-within-a-tale similar to Conrad's, distances the reader and makes it difficult to pin down authorial attitudes. The story also contains some interesting self-reflexive images: the male first-person narrator of the inset tale describes his cousin Bob beside the dead Indian "standing there in his shabby khaki and frayed putties, as much an embodiment of the Empire as if he were in gold-laced uniform and stiff with medals and orders!" (pp. 327–8).

I would not want to make extravagant claims for this story, but I would suggest that Violet Jacob's writings concerning India, like those, no doubt, of other Scots involved in Empire, merit attention both for their intrinsic interest, and for the light they shed on an aspect of Scottish experience that has not, in its literary expression, been widely considered or placed in relation to other aspects of our culture: perhaps because it does not necessarily always reflect too well on us. The Canadian writer Margaret Atwood has commented in relation to her own country:

> I have always seen Canadian nationalism and the con-cern for women's rights as part of a larger non-exclusive picture. We sometimes forget, in our obsession with col-onialism and imperialism, that Canada itself has been guilty of these stances towards others, both inside the country and outside it.[14]

Such a view might have resonances in other places.

Violet Jacob is a writer whose work yields much if we are prepared to look seriously at her texts. Obviously, in a limited space I have only glanced at her prose, and much work remains to be done. The limitations of critical response to her so far arise partly from ignorance – so much of her work is out of print and unread – but suggest also the need for a pluralistic criticism of Scottish literature that is open to the potentialities of work done by writers with varied interests and varied attitudes to their homeland. In particular, we need to look again at our women writers, so many of whom have sunk into undeserved oblivion and been undervalued and even denigrated. Like many other female fiction writers and poets (and writers in other genres) Violet Jacob is due for "debate", both in the English sense of "discussion" or "dispute", and in the slightly different (and stronger?) Scots sense of "fight" or "defence". Scotland, that small but most debateable of lands, needs to look again – and again – at its own traditions.

Bibliography of Books Published by Violet Jacob

The Baillie MacPhee (a poem), by Walter Douglas Campbell and Violet Kennedy-Erskine, William Blackwood, Edinburgh and London, 1888, with illustrations by Violet Kennedy-Erskine.

The Sheepstealers, William Heinemann, London, 1902, a novel.

The Infant Moralist (verses), by Lady Helena Carnegie and Mrs Arthur Jacob, R. Grant and Son, Edinburgh, and R. Brimley Johnson, London, 1903, with illustrations by Mrs Arthur Jacob.

The Interloper, William Heinemann, London, 1904, a novel.

The Golden Heart and Other Fairy Stories, William Heinemann, London, 1904.

Verses, William Heinemann, London, 1904.

Irresolute Catherine, John Murray, London, 1908, a novel.

The History of Aythan Waring, William Heinemann, London, 1908, a novel.

Stories Told by the Miller, John Murray, London, 1909, for children.

The Fortune Hunters and Other Stories, John Murray, London, 1910.

Flemington, John Murray, London, 1911, a novel.

Songs of Angus, John Murray, London, 1915, poems.

More Songs of Angus and Others, Country Life/George Newnes, London, and Charles Scribner's Sons, New York, 1918, poems.

Bonnie Joann and Other Poems, John Murray, London, 1921.

Tales of My Own Country, John Murray, London, 1922.

Two New Poems: "Rohallion" and "The Little Dragon", Porpoise Press, Edinburgh, 1924.

The Northern Lights and Other Poems, John Murray, London, 1927.

The Good Child's Year Book, Foulis, London, 1928, with illustrations by Violet Jacob.

The Lairds of Dun, John Murray, London, 1931, a history of the Erskine family.

The Scottish Poems of Violet Jacob, Oliver & Boyd, Edinburgh, 1944.

The Lum Hat and Other Stories: Last Tales of Violet Jacob, edited by Ronald Garden, Aberdeen University Press, Aberdeen, 1982.

Diaries and Letters from India 1895–1900, edited by Carol Anderson, Canongate, Edinburgh, 1990.

There are also stories and articles in journals.

Contemporary Feminist Fantasy in the Scottish Literary Tradition

Margaret Elphinstone

Much of the fantasy currently written by Scottish women draws on a strong but not immediately obvious tradition in Scottish literature. I first became aware of this radical use of traditional themes through the critical reception of my own fiction, but realized that it had wider implications for the work of other contemporary Scottish women authors.

It is not easy for writers to assess their own use of tradition. When, for example, I began writing short stories I found that certain supernatural elements began to recur: in an early story, "Spinning the Green", I was using traditional tales in a response to a contemporary situation. In the early eighties, moved, and somewhat confused, by visits to Greenham Common, I worked out a story which was a deliberate composite pastiche, using Beauty and the Beast, *Alice in Wonderland*[1] and the tales of Robin Hood. In terms of parody, I thought I knew what I was doing; the only result that surprised me was that The Women's Press published it in an anthology of science fiction.[2]

The paradox has not been resolved. My first novel, *The Incomer*,[3] was also placed on The Women's Press science fiction list. Flattered, but also puzzled, I considered the fact that, as far as I knew, I never read science fiction. I thought I had written a novel which drew its imagery from the Galloway countryside and folk tradition. I thought I was writing about where I lived. Certainly I had transposed my own village into another world, but it was not one that seemed alien to me. In questioning the definition placed on my own work, I found myself dragged into the apparently insoluble controversy concerning what constitutes science fiction. I read my own reviews, some of which criticized me for failing to write real science fiction. (When I saw myself described as a feminist Luddite, on the whole I could only agree.) Reading further, I found that two writers I much admired also stood accused: Marge Piercy and Ursula Le Guin. Certainly I could acknowledge a debt to American feminist fantasy, but I didn't think this was the whole story.

Thus began a quest for sources that led me back into academic criticism, and then into a more remote past, both personal and literary. I was given two major clues. The first was offered by Douglas Gifford, whose review specifically related my work to the Scottish literary tradition. The second was from Polygon, who published my next novel[4] (set in exactly the same world as the first) under the title of Scottish fantasy. The redefinitions that followed opened up new areas of discovery. Firstly, I had not properly considered Scottish literature as an entity, still less as a formative influence. My study of English literature at an English university had never suggested such a thing. Secondly, it had not previously occurred to me how much of my early, and most significant, reading, was in fact Scottish literature. I grew up on Macdonald, Stevenson, and Scott, among the novelists, and on Burns, Hogg, and the ballads by way of poetry, and also on a wealth of folk tale and folk tradition. My debt to my grandparents' old-fashioned library is that I had access to Scottish literature years before I ever heard of it.

I began to try to identify those awkward tendencies in my work which seemed to exclude it from the genre, science fiction, feminist or otherwise. It seemed to me there were four major differences, all of which I had seen developed and exploited by Scottish writers of far greater stature than I could aspire to be.

Firstly, place is paramount. It is the connecting factor between this world and the other. Real places, often a real Scotland, remain identifiable in the fantastic world. Macdonald's country of goblins and princesses has unmistakable features of Grampian.[5] Hogg's background for Michael Scott's traffic with the devil is the real Aikwood, set in the real Borders. One can follow the fantastic journeys in *The Three Perils of Man*[6] on foot, with the book in one hand and the Ordnance Survey map in the other.

Secondly, the other world is often as much historical as it is fantastic. The fact that in twentieth-century renderings it is often set in a supposed future is almost immaterial. Scottish literature not only developed the marriage of the supernatural with a pragmatic realism, from the ballads onward, it also produced the historical novel, out of a philosophy of history that was fully aware that historical accounts are merely points of view. Both Scott and Hogg introduce fantastic elements into their versions of a historical past. Their contemporary, Galt, in *Ringan Gilhaize*,[7] uses madness rather than fantasy as the lens through which historical event is refracted. And of course the ballads themselves often embody folk history.

Thirdly, the ballads and the folk tradition have survived in literature, against all competition from other sources and other media. Hogg's mother was partly right when she warned Scott that if he wrote her ballads down, he would destroy them so that they would never be told again. But the written collections, from Ramsay's onwards, also preserved the past, and unashamedly transmuted it into new forms. This particular strand of Scottish literature has weathered sentimentality, and is still available to contemporary writers.

Finally, a significant part of the Scottish heritage for women writers now is the figure of the dangerous woman. In twentieth-century writing she may sometimes seem to align herself with a feminist perspective, but she refuses to become quite ideologically sound. She is too sinister for that. She has appeared since the ballads as the daughter of the other world, with all the danger and glamour that that implies. In modern fantasy her refusal to accommodate herself to a world of known boundaries and social realism may be related to her psychological alienation from the patriarchal model. But with the other world open to her, she becomes more than subversive, she is perilous, and perhaps, in terms of accepted moralities, downright evil. She has a long and questionable history.

*

There is an illuminating comparison to be made between two first novels by Scottish women writers, both published in 1989. The first, by Janice Galloway, *The Trick is to Keep Breathing*,[8] attracted four British awards, including the MIND award for the novel of the year that has done most to alleviate the oppression of those suffering mental illness. The book concerns a teacher in Ayrshire whose unfulfilled external life, and developing fantasy life, leads to what is, in social terms, a mental breakdown. The novel reflects her gradual fragmentation in terms of plot, characterization, and language. The second novel, by Sian Hayton, *Cells of Knowledge*,[9] won the Scottish First Book of the Year award from the Saltire Society. It concerns a giant's daughter living in the tenth century, and is also set in south-west Scotland. Marighal's magical powers make her uncontrollable and terrible in the world of the Celtic Christian monks, in spite of her manifest goodwill and state of grace. Through a text written by two Christian narrators, we see the fragmentation of the Christian patriarchy and, ironically inferred, the construction of its opposite.

Both books are set in south-west Scotland. Both deal with states of mind. Both focus upon the ironic construction of a subversive female vision through the text of a patriarchal world. But only Hayton turns to a Scottish past, and takes magic and folktale and makes it contemporary, both in terms of psychological analysis and in her use of the fantasy genre. Thus she creates a more subversive alternative than Galloway, whose heroine, stuck in contemporary Ayrshire, can go no further than madness.

Scottish literature has always shown a predilection for exploring psychological state in terms of fantasy. Perhaps the first critic to define the Scottish method of combining the supernatural with psychological and social realism was Gregory Smith, in his book *Scottish Literature*, published in 1919.[10] It was he who coined the expression "the polar twins of the Scottish Muse", to describe the juxtaposition of what he names "the prose of extravagance" (fantasy), and the prose of experience (the pragmatic). Scottish literature is often characterized by violent fluctuations between the two. Rather than discuss this paradigm in the light of later critical theory, I would like to consider how it relates to certain Scottish texts, and thereby prove its efficacy. In particular, I shall look at certain texts considered by Smith that bear direct relation to contemporary Scottish women's writing.

First, an obvious and often explicit source is the ballads, particularly the body of ballads dealing with the magical and the supernatural. Dangerous women are a feature of many of these ballads, and in their actions they tend to take control over both the marvellous and the practical in a striking manner. In *Lamkin*[11] for example, we have the "fause nourice", who lends a sinister aid to Lamkin when he destroys her lady and her nursling, and who also attends to important details, like bringing a bowl in which to catch the blood. The Faerie Queen of *True Thomas*,[11] is a highly sexual being from a supernatural realm, who takes Thomas into another world, and also sees that he gets a new suit of clothes. These women belong in a world that is both fantastic, and subject to practical and domestic details. Their emotions are ordinary, their sphere of operation magical. The result is a double-edged power. We see this clearly in Margret of *Tam Lin*.[11] She wins her man back by holding on to him as the Faerie Queen turns him from one shape into another. The shape-changing is marvellous, but at the last line of every stanza, we see that her motivation behind it is recognizable, ordinary and universal:

> He grew into her arms two
>   Like to a savage wild;
> She held him fast, let him not go,
>   The father of her child
>
> He grew into her arms two
>   Like an adder or a snake;
> She held him fast, let him not go,
>   He was her earthly maick [*mate*].
>
> He grew into her arms two
>   Like iron in hot fire
> She held him fast, let him not go,
>   He was her heart's desire. (p. 100)

Many of today's fantasy writers are quite explicit in their use of the ballads; they quote them directly, and make use of their plots and narrative techniques. I shall discuss some of them later.

The same stark mixture of the ordinary and the marvellous occurs in much Scottish poetry, and subsequently takes over in the Scottish novel of the nineteenth century. In the novels of Sir Walter Scott, we find, in a predominantly naturalistic world, fantastic outcast characters, and embedded tales like Wandering Willie's tale in *Redgauntlet*.[12] But the two Scottish novels of the nineteenth century which have most clearly influenced modern feminist writing in Scotland, are undoubtedly *The Private Memoirs and Confessions of a Justified Sinner* by James Hogg,[13] published in 1824, and *The Strange Case of Dr. Jekyll and Mr. Hyde* by Robert Louis Stevenson, published in 1886.[14]

In the novel, the familiar juxtaposition of the prose of extravagance and the prose of experience has become internalized. The unanswered question of *The Private Memoirs and Confessions of a Justified Sinner* is, is this a novel of psychological realism, giving us a clinical study of madness, or an account of the possession of a man by a real devil, an external battle for souls in a world that is both recognizable and historically specific, yet also inhabited by supernatural agencies? It is, of course, both; Hogg allows no single answer.

Like Hogg, Stevenson, in *The Strange Case of Dr. Jekyll and Mr. Hyde*, focuses upon the fantastic externalization of an internal conflict. The book has achieved mythic status in its delineation of the divided self, itself a constant preoccupation of Scottish literature. R.D. Laing was not a Scot for nothing. Thus, in the prose of extravagance, we have devils and sorcerers; in the prose of experience we have (to be anachronistic for a moment) schizophrenia.

In contemporary feminist fantasy, we can see clearly how the traditional Scottish treatment of internal conflict, madness, and the divided self, provides an excellent literary tradition for the Scottish woman writer. The use of the fantastic in this country has been less to create Utopias than to explore the divided psyche through the use of the marvellous. Supernatural agencies and other worlds become vehicles for the expression of a fragmented psychological state.

It is interesting, for example, that Liz Lochhead, in her

play *Dracula*,[15] names and uses a Gothic model to explore the conflict between the outward "good" woman and the inner, amoral self who is not touched by social values, and whose expression must be seen paradoxically as both liberation and destruction. Mina, going with the "good" men to destroy Count Dracula in his castle, expresses her social self and vampire self in one speech:

> "You fed me oranges; I smelt the peel, spat out the pips, but all the time I tasted blood. . . . I was already here alone on the high crag of my castle and when you, my husband, held me tight and tethered to the earth in strange bed after strange bed, while you slept I flew wild and free in the night." (p. 144)

Of the recent Scottish feminist novels containing images of the fragmented or suppressed self, I would like now to take four examples, in order to show how they acknowledge and develop the Scottish literary tradition.

Emma Tennant's *Two Women of London*[16] uses the juxtaposition of the recognizable and the bizarre familiar to us from the ballads. She makes a more obvious and explicit link with Stevenson: the subtitle of the novel is *The Strange Case of Ms Jekyll and Mrs Hyde*. Like Lochhead, Tennant does not hesitate to name her sources. Like Stevenson, she uses a London background that suggests Edinburgh, and she makes close approximations to Stevenson's story. Mrs Hyde, dreadful in her plastic mackintosh, is a downtrodden, embittered single mother who commits murder, while Ms Jekyll is a successful, unencumbered woman, who turns out to be a predator upon the vitality of Mrs Hyde. But the symbiosis goes much further than social comment, although this is undoubtedly present. In constructing a model of a divided self, Tennant shows her usual ability to create a brooding atmosphere of Gothic horror.

Fragmentation goes further than in her original. Interestingly, Hastie Lanyon, the doctor in Stevenson's narrative who witnesses Jekyll's transformation, and dies of the shock, has been replaced by two characters. Jean Hastie is from Scotland, and is researching a work of gynocriticism, *In the Garden*. Dr Frances Crane is the one who dies of shock. Jean Hastie is a survivor, who has affinities with Mrs Hyde herself: both are preoccupied with motherhood, and they bear a physical resemblance to one another.

There are other obvious allusions in names. Ms Jekyll's servant is called Grace Poole. The madwoman has shifted from *Jane Eyre*'s attic to Mrs Hyde's child-ridden cellar. The book shares with Tennant's *The Bad Sister*,[17] (equally overtly based on Hogg's *The Private Memoirs and Confessions of a Justified Sinner*) an ambiguous attitude to the group of apparently liberated middle-class women. Although they constitute themselves collective enemies of Mrs Hyde, in so far as she threatens their whole being simply by existing, they also need her, and feed off her. The conflict, of course, is internal, as she is a part of each one of them. Ms Jekyll is not alone in having an *alter ego* who is not only a murderer of men, but, worse still, lewd and ugly. We first meet Mrs Hyde at the opening of Mara Kaletsky's exhibition, in which Mara has made a collage of the women's faces cut up and stuck together. They amount to Mrs Hyde, as Mara tells us:

> "Now look at my canvases. I shoot film of all the women and I intercut the stills so I get the ultimate woman. You don't like that one? Who is it? It's the Face of Revenge."
> (p. 12)

When she films Mrs Hyde, we see the dissolution of a once noble face, and again Mara comments:

> "the extreme unease experienced by all the women in their different ways when confronted by this spectacle is due to there being something 'unnatural' about Mrs Hyde." (p. 32)

It is upon this fragmentation that Ms Jekyll's beauty is constructed, just as her upmarket house is built upon Mrs Hyde's rotting basement, a juxtaposition Jean Hastie describes in her journal as "surreal – if that's the word".

Like Hogg and Stevenson, Tennant sets her novel in a surreal present time; Sian Hayton, in *Cells of Knowledge*, places the conflict of the divided self in a magical past. There is much to say about this book, but for my present purpose I will focus upon one episode, in which Marighal, in order to save the life of Kynan, to whom she is betrothed, dies at his hand and is sacrificed, so that he can perform the task the giant, her father, sets him, on which his life depends. Marighal stage-manages her own death and resurrection in an act of extraordinary power. Her lover has to decapitate her, dismember her, and reassemble her bones, reciting the spell she has taught him, while he obeys her instructions to the letter. The monk's marginal comment points out the blasphemy of a woman's taking on the sacrificial role of saviour that is a male God's prerogative.

Unfortunately Marighal's plan miscarries in so far as two Marighals come back to life, as she describes:

"behold, there was a double of myself, gazing at me with eyes as empty as a newborn child." (p. 159)

The shell of Marighal, her second self, is found by Kynan, who marries her, relieved to find that she has forgotten her magical powers and her terrible supernatural past. She grows fat and timid under his protection, while the prototype Marighal, purged of all weakness, seeks single-mindedly for grace, demanding neither support nor pity. Over the years the two Marighals, once identical, change utterly in response to their separate roles.

Marighal and her numerous sisters are the immortal daughters of the giant Uthebhan. They are outside human society, beyond the pale of both Christianity and patriarchy, and so their strength, although accompanied by wisdom and goodwill, can only be perceived by Christian men as a threat. Uthebhan's rule spells terror for mortal men, but invests his daughters with magical powers, including, as we saw, power over death itself. The daughters owe their lives to the deaths of mortal women, for their mothers inevitably die in giving birth to the giant's progeny. Reconciled to patriarchy and purged of strength, Marighal's shadow becomes a travesty of her other self.

With the killing of the giant, and the acceptance of Christianity, the daughters of the giant become mortal. But the giant still haunts men's dreams. The last words of the book are his, as he speaks in a dream to the monk Selyf, who is sleeping on the giant's death stone:

> "You do well to lie on our death stone, mortal man, for it speaks to you of your corruptibility. I kept my daughters confined here so that they would not change and be perverted into the monsters I had seen out in the world. Yet in spite of my strength and wisdom, I could not sustain my role forever . . . .
>
> But whenever mankind forget [*sic*] my daughters, the clever, the kind and the wise, I will come forth and walk the world again, and I will increase their sorrow a thousand-fold." (p. 197)

In fantasy, past and future are often closely allied. Turning from the tenth century to an undefined future, I would like now to look at Naomi Mitchison's *Memoirs of a Spacewoman*,[18] first published in 1962, and once again to select the episode which deals most overtly with the divided self in relation to women in society. In this section, an all-women space team explores a planet chiefly inhabited by giant caterpillars and butterflies. The butterflies hate the apparently guileless caterpillars, and overshadow them by projections of unbearable guilt and fear. The caterpillars literally collapse under the oppressive weight of these feelings. Slowly the spacewomen discover why the caterpillars threaten the existence of the butterflies. The caterpillars copulate in the swamps of the strange planet, and so cause the butterflies to give birth, and in so doing, die. The butterflies believe themselves to be immortal, if not forced to procreate.

The caterpillars are endearing, and one of the women takes their part, and commits the unforgivable crime of interference. She kills a butterfly, to prove that it is false that, free from their reproductive role, the butterflies would be immortal. But the leader of the team is enchanted by the vision of the butterflies. Like the creatures themselves, we see the women torn between compassion for the physically ordinary, and delight in the marvellous which feeds off and negates the value of the merely ordinary. Once again the division, finally, is within.

Naomi Mitchison has also written extensively about a Scottish past, and her futuristic science fiction is not unconnected with her historical fiction. In particular, her spacewoman, Mary, has affinities with the Scottish witch of the historical past. Like the devil, and often associated with him, the Scottish witch remains a powerful symbol. The Scottish Reformation destroyed the cult of Mary in Scotland, as well as being the downfall of Mary, Queen of Scots, and was followed by some of the latest and most comprehensive witch hunts in Europe. In later Scottish fiction, we sometimes find echoes of the older, pagan, Faerie Queen, both sinister and attractive, who seduces True Thomas:

> All hail, thou mighty Queen of Heaven!
>   For your peer on earth I never did see.

> O no, o no, True Thomas, she says,
>   That name does not belong to me
> I am but the Queen of fair Elfland
>   And I'm come here for to visit thee. (p. 25)[4]

In contemporary feminist fiction, we find this figure has taken on a new role. It is interesting in this respect that Mitchison turns from the ambivalent figure of Kirstie, in *The Bull Calves*,[19] set in the eighteenth century, to Mary, her Spacewoman of the future. In Kirstie, who has dabbled in witchcraft and whose first marriage is a scandal, Mitchison shows a woman transgressing her traditional role, at a time when conformity to patriarchy could be enforced by a husband, or, failing that, the Kirk. We see that Kirstie steps outside the roles that are safe for her in her time, but she has explicitly to deny power even while she has it, for example, to her niece Catherine:

"Aunt Kirstie, do you believe at all in witches and that?"

"Ach no, it is the evil in folks turning against themselves and others. Whether it is there by original sin or put there by the De'il when folks' lives get so that he can edge himself among them and spoil the good that should be there. And dinna you get believing in witches, Catherine, even if you must have your castles and enchantments and knights in armour! Witchcraft was a gey ugly thing, whatever made it; And it is over and done with in Scotland for ever." (p. 91)

But ironically, we discover that Kirstie has been in danger; she has transgressed the bounds of her society. Thus we learn *why* she needs to disbelieve in witchcraft, whereas for young, untried Catherine there has been no struggle.

The same pressure to conform to normality, or sanity, appears in the future world of *Memoirs of a Spacewoman*. Mitchison has transposed the same question from the past to the future. To be allowed to explore in space, it is necessary to give proof of what is referred to throughout the text as "a stable personality". But for Mary, writing her memoirs at the end of a long career, the question is not that simple. She knows now that transgression is always inevitable, indeed necessary, and that there is no such thing as non-interference:

It always seems to me curious that there are some things in exploration that we simply cannot think will happen, in spite of all our warnings and examples. A failure of communication? Or imagination? Does communication wipe out imagination, which is, in a sense, solitary? . . . the difficulty seems to be that in the nursery world we take ourselves for granted as stable personalities, as completely secure. Impossible that we should ever deviate, that interference should ever be a temptation. Not for us, we think! How young can one be! (p. 19)

Finally, I would like to consider the recent fiction of Muriel Spark in the light of these themes. A Scottish writer who has often moved far from Scotland, Spark retains a surreal, often macabre element in her fiction which owes its origins to the Scottish tradition. Alan Bold gives a useful analysis of Spark as a Scottish writer, and concludes:

The influence of James Hogg's *The Private Memoirs and Confessions of a Justified Sinner* and Stevenson's *The Strange Case of Dr. Jekyll and Mr. Hyde* must have made profound impressions on a writer fascinated by the coexistence of good and evil. Above all, though, the ballads helped to shape Spark's prose with its timeshifts, its combination of the natural and supernatural, its atmosphere of enchantment. (p. 26)[20]

The witch, or woman of power, features strongly in Spark's most recent novel, *Symposium*,[21] 1990. It is interesting that in some of Spark's earlier novels, this figure has become centred upon the author herself. In all her work, Spark deals with deceit and double meanings, in words, sentences and narratives. We see characters judged according to the integrity of the narratives they create for themselves. In this respect, it is the assumption of authority itself that becomes suspect, a nice development of the question of authorial responsibility. In Spark's first novel, *The Comforters*,[22] we see Caroline Rose haunted by the shade of her own author, as she hears the ghostly typewriter in the next room, and realizes that she is a character in someone else's novel, but is also the author of her own life. Twenty-four years later, in *Loitering with Intent*,[23] we see Fleur Talbot writing her novel, which becomes both cause and effect of reality. The book becomes a surreal form of autobiography, an exploration of the power of the author that is both joyful and sinister.

Symposium marks the first return to a Scottish theme since *The Prime of Miss Jean Brodie*,[24] in 1961. Margaret Murchie comes from a Scottish family dominated by mad Uncle Magnus, who quotes the ballads as he takes charge of lives and deaths. Through marriage, she erupts into a London circle of the pragmatic, rich, and content, just as Dougal once erupted into Peckham Rye.[25] Margaret has the disconcerting power of bringing about sudden death by the mere fact of her presence. Her moral responsibility for this uncanny knack becomes the dominating question of the novel. Her parents are terrified of her; Uncle Magnus recognizes a kindred spirit in the words of the ballads:

Uncle Magnus greeted Margaret with the words:

"O was it a wer-wolf in the wood
  Or was it a mermaid in the sea
Or was it a man or vile woman
  My true love that mis-shapit thee?" (p. 141)

Margaret fixes her evil eye upon her mother-in-law, Hilda
Damien, but other perpetrators of violent crime forestall her.
This dislocation of her own authority unhinges Margaret, who
finally gives herself away. Hilda is killed on a Friday, and
when the police arrive with the news: "From upstairs came
Margaret's wild cry: 'It shouldn't have been till Sunday!' "

Spark is of course justly famed for her use of irony, and
the economy and wit of her narrative technique. However, a
fine use of irony is common to all the writers I have mentioned.
It is fair to say that Tennant owes her mastery of ironic
method partly to the influence of Spark, as a review in *Scotland
on Sunday* points out: "*Two Women of London* is reminiscent of
Muriel Spark at her very darkest and very best." Sian Hayton's technique is very different, but works to similar ironic
effect. Her story of a pagan giant's daughter is told through
the dual narrative of two Celtic Christian monks. The second
narrative exists literally as glosses upon the first, and at the
end we find the commentator is the son as well as the spiritual
heir of the original author. So we have to reach the truth
through two distorting lenses, in two male Christian narratives
that quite fail to fathom the meaning of their subject matter.
Thus we get the same sense of unnatural containment that
we find in Mitchison's *The Bull Calves*, where we see that
Kirstie, in eighteenth-century Scotland, cannot tell the whole
truth. Nor, indeed, can the spacewoman, Mary, who also has
to write within the mores of her élite society of space travellers;
however, she too creates a more subversive narrative through
ironic self-revelation.

In other words, these authors require us to read the
spaces, and attend to what, within the bounds of patriarchy
or the assumptions of a dominating group, cannot be said. I
would suggest that here too we find a link with the Scottish
tradition. As we see in the examples of the ballads, of Hogg,

and of Stevenson, in Scottish literature we are constantly invited to go beyond the fragmentation of language, nationality, and culture, and to read the unstated narrative. In present-day Scottish women authors we can now see the same tradition developed and turned to new purposes, in terms of contemporary feminist fantasy.

Parents and Children

"Exactly Them Words":
Histories of a Murderous Daughter

Caroline Gonda

In an engraving from the mid eighteenth century, two women sit by the fire, drinking tea and chatting. The little tea-chest on the table, open to reveal its canisters, reminds us that in this period tea is still a luxury, a precious commodity to be kept under lock and key. Sitting proprietorially by the tea-table, the more elaborately dressed of the two women looks as if she is at home with such luxury. But a closer inspection shows that this decorous scene is not what it seems, that the lady with the teapot is not, literally, at home. The leg-irons beneath her hoop and gown, the bars on the window, instruct us that, in a different sense, this woman, too, is precious, must be kept under lock and key. For this, the engraving's caption tells us, is "Miss Mary Blandy, in Oxford Castle Goal [*sic*], charged with the Cruel Murder of her Father, Mr. Francis Blandy, late of Henley upon Thames in Oxfordshire, by Puting [*sic*] Poison into his Water Gruel, 1751."[1]

On 6th April 1752, Mary Blandy was hanged for the murder of her father.

The newspapers and magazines covered the execution – as they had done the trial – at some length, but they were by no means the only sources of information about the case. Indeed, one of the most fascinating things about Mary

Blandy's story, for a twentieth-century reader, is the bewildering variety of versions in which that story exists: in poetry, prose, and drama; in polemical tracts and trial proceedings; in official letters between ministers of state, indignant letters to the magazines, and gossipy letters between intimate friends. The story travels in pamphlets and broadsheets, in prints and caricature; in versions from the spurious (Original Letters and Genuine Lives) to the frankly fantastic (Miss Blandy's last message from Hell).

Even before the trial, the printed attacks on Mary Blandy had already reached such a pitch that the defence had requested permission to call Mr Swinton, the chaplain who had attended Mary in prison, as an additional character witness. The judge had refused, saying that the jury would, of course, disregard all such publications and look only at the evidence presented in court. For readers who did not attend the trial, even looking at the evidence has its own complications, since the trial proceedings themselves exist in different forms: the more official version, published in London "by Permission of the Judges", presents itself as dialogue, with the name of each speaker in the margin; but the version published in Edinburgh, which consists mainly of paraphrase and reported speech, differs from it in significant details, including the date of the trial itself.[2]

Those eager to hear Mary's own side of the story could buy her *Narrative*, written in the hopes of attracting Royal clemency, though they would have to wait until 10th April before spending one shilling and sixpence on *Miss Mary Blandy's Own Account* (expensive, but three times as long). To prove these accounts genuine, original documents, "in Miss Blandy's own Hand-Writing", or "authenticated by Miss *Blandy* in a proper Manner", had been deposited with the publisher in each case "for the Satisfaction of the Public"; moreover the *Account*, published "at her dying Request", included a copy of the declaration "signed by herself, in the Presence of two Clergymen, two Days before her Execution".[3] Even after Mary Blandy's death, the pamphlet war continued for almost a year: there were Authentic, Full, Secret and Genuine Histories; a separate reprint of the Hon. Mr Bathurst's opening speech for the Crown; even a three-act tragedy (never performed), "founded on a late melancholy Event" and entitled *The Fair Parricide*.[4]

Accounts of the case not only appear in different forms, in different contexts and at different social levels: they are also prompted by different motives, from money-making to survival; they offer a variety of explanations; and they find very little on which to agree. With so many versions to choose from, the task of disentangling the truth about Mary Blandy is not an easy one.

The undisputed facts of the case are these: Mary Blandy was the only child of a well-off attorney from Henley, who let it be known that his daughter would have £10,000 on her marriage. A Scottish officer, Captain the Hon. William-Henry Cranstoun, fifth son of a Scots peer, and grandson of the Marquis of Lothian, met Mary in 1746 and began courting her soon after. She was already in her mid twenties and still unmarried. He, on the other hand, already had a wife and child – or, as he assured the Blandys when the news broke, a mistress and bastard – living in Scotland. Despite this entanglement, Cranstoun continued to court Mary, with her father's permission and her mother's encouragement, while the question of his marital status was being decided in the Scottish courts. He also stayed with the Blandys for months at a time, even after Mrs Blandy's death in 1749.

On 5th August 1751, some nine months after Cranstoun had returned to Scotland from his last visit, Mr Blandy was taken ill, and died on the 14th, after several days in great pain. He had been eating water-gruel (a thin porridge made with oatmeal and water) which was subsequently found to contain arsenic. Mary was arrested as a result of detective work by the servants, and by the eminent Dr Addington, who had attended Mr Blandy in the last stages of his illness. Their evidence at the trial, including the results of Dr Addington's post-mortem on Mr Blandy, outweighed Mary's few witnesses and her own appeal to the jury (since a defending counsel was not allowed to address the jury directly, the prisoner customarily made her or his own speech for the defence). Mary Blandy never denied that she had put the fatal powder into the water-gruel: she simply insisted that Cranstoun had sent it to her, telling her it was a harmless "love-powder" which would make Mr Blandy look kindly on his prospective son-in-law – and that she had believed Cranstoun's story. Her own story did not convince the jury, who took five minutes to find her guilty; nor did it bring her the reprieve she had hoped for. She was executed at Oxford, aged thirty-three.

Cranstoun had escaped to Calais, a fortnight after Mary's arrest, profiting by the confusion as to who, in England, should or could issue a warrant to arrest a man residing in Scotland. He was never brought to trial, but did not long outlive Mary: he died in late November or early December 1752, at an inn, the Burgundy Cross, at Furnes, near Dunkirk. Accounts of his death agree that he was so swollen that it was expected he would burst; that he died in great torments; that he was converted to Catholicism on his deathbed; and that he always insisted Mary Blandy was not as innocent as she had claimed.[5]

Cranstoun's conversion provides a fittingly ironic conclusion to his story, since religion, and Catholicism in particular, had played a significant part in his marital history. In 1744 Cranstoun had privately married a Miss Anne Murray, but, as the Murrays were Jacobites and Catholics, the Presbyterian Cranstoun insisted that the marriage be kept a family secret, for fear it would block his promotion. Cranstoun had joined the army under Butcher Cumberland, on what, in the months of the '45, must often have seemed the wrong side for a Scot. Moreover, Anne was not only from a Jacobite family, she was also the niece of John Murray of Broughton, the secretary to Prince Charles, the Young Pretender. Anne became pregnant, and was invited to stay at the Cranstoun family seat by her mother-in-law, Lady Cranstoun; apparently fearing that Presbyterian influence would be brought to bear on her, she declined the invitation.

After the child's birth, and after the trial of Anne's brother for his part in the '45, Cranstoun claimed that he had proposed marriage to Anne when she was already his mistress, but only on condition that she turn Presbyterian. Since she had refused to do so, he claimed, he was under no further obligation to her. Following Scottish law, Anne raised an action of declarator of marriage in the Commissary Court at Edinburgh in October 1756. Cranstoun, finding that his great-uncle, Lord Mark Ker (at whose house he'd first met Mary), had given the game away to the Blandys, while the action was still pending in 1747, insisted that any contract between himself and Miss Murray arose purely from cohabitation and was therefore invalid under English law. Even after the Court found for Anne in March 1748, ordering him to pay a combined annual maintenance of £50 sterling for her and the child, and finding him liable for expenses; and even when Anne wrote to the Blandys enclosing a copy of the Court's decree, Cranstoun simply lodged an appeal with the Court of Sessions and went on denying the marriage.

Bizarre as all this seems, it is nevertheless true that Scottish marriage law during this period was confusing, to the Scots as well as to the English. One writer in the 1770s observed:

> Even an Englishman looks upon the solemnization of [marriage] as a serious thing: but here, it is a matter of merriment, and no ceremony at all is necessary. A man, indeed, in Scotland, can scarce be said to know whether he is married or not, as his own consent is no part of the business.[6]

Proof of cohabitation would not in itself, as Cranstoun claimed, be proof of marriage; even "marriage by habit and repute" – the truth behind the myth that "In Scotland you're married if people think you are" – required that the parties should cohabit *and* pass as married for a considerable length of time.[7] The Cranstouns' private marriage would have been a marriage by declaration, i.e. a pronouncement by the couple themselves, which did not have to be solemnized by the Church, or even witnessed by third parties, in order to be valid. Proving marriage by declaration could indeed be difficult if one partner was unable or unwilling to testify. William Roughead, the twentieth-century editor of the Blandy trial for Hodge's Notable English Trials series, and himself a Scottish lawyer (Writer to the Signet), notes that in this case Cranstoun's own letters told against him, including the covering letter and draft for a declaration he had persuaded Anne to write stating that she was not married to him; when Cranstoun

produced the declaration in Anne's writing, Anne produced
the originals in *his*. As a Catholic and Jacobite woman, Anne
Murray, representative of a disadvantaged minority, proved
better able to cope with the Hon. William-Henry Cranstoun
than did her more sheltered English counterpart, Mary
Blandy.

Mary Blandy was, to all appearances, surrounded by
legal advisers: her father was an attorney; her maternal uncle,
Mr Serjeant Stevens, a successful barrister, with chambers at
Doctors' Commons in London (unlike his brother-in-law, he
always refused to receive Cranstoun).[8] Given the poor com-
munications between England and Scotland, and the uncertainty about what constituted a valid marriage under Scottish
law, however, it is perhaps not so surprising that Cranstoun
thought he could get away with it – and did. The English
Blandys might readily believe in Scotland as a land of barbarous moral and legal confusion; but Cranstoun's Scotland, as
he presented it, was also a place of magic, mystery, and
superstition. Cranstoun claimed to have got his "love-powder"
from Mrs Morgan, a famous cunning-woman in Edinburgh;
he talked of seeing the ghost of the still living Mr Blandy, and
of hearing supernatural music in the Blandys' house. (Mr
Blandy, not best pleased to find Cranstoun regaling his daughter and servants with these tales, remarked that he supposed
it was "Scotch Music".) Finally, Scotland was the place from
which lavish gifts arrived: a box of table linen, or a kippered
salmon, from the Marquis of Lothian's daughter, Lady Cranstoun; and for Mary, from Cranstoun himself, a box of "*Scotch*
Pebbles", to be set as ornaments – the height of fashion in
jewellery in 1751.

At Mary's trial the Crown would produce a packet,
marked "The Powder to clean the Pebbles", which Mary had
tried to burn in the kitchen fire during her father's fatal illness,
a packet rescued by the maids, Susannah Gunnell and Betty
Binfield. Gunnell and Binfield, growing suspicious of Mary's
visits to the gruel-pan in the pantry, had already found a
gritty, white sediment in the bottom of the pan, and had
taken both container and contents to the house of Mary's
godmother, Mrs Mounteney, for the apothecary to analyse.
There was not enough powder left in the packet to make

a satisfactory analysis of that, but Dr Addington (who had conducted the tests on the gruel, as well as the post-mortem on Mr Blandy) testified that he believed that it, too, was white arsenic. A caricature of the time, "The Scotch Triumvirate", reproduced in William Roughead's *Trial of Mary Blandy* (facing p. 208), shows Cranstoun with a paper sticking out of his pocket, marked "Powder to clean Pebbels" [*sic*], and another at his feet, advertising "Scotch Powder to cure the Itch". The ghost of Mary Blandy, trying to cover her body, which is exposed to the waist by her shroud, says "My Honour, Cra— — —s ruin'd me", while the ghost of Mrs Blandy says "Child he's Married!" Cranstoun, with a rope around his neck and slung like a sash across his body, says confidently "Jammy will save me" (Jammy is presumably his older brother James, sixth Lord Cranstoun).

Cranstoun was saved, though not for long; but his escape clearly made things harder on Mary. Roughead quotes a letter from the Chancellor, Lord Hardwicke, to the Duke of Newcastle, noting that Cranstoun's escape "may create some clamour", and asking whether this may not "be a further reason for the Government shewing a more than ordinary attention to ye Prosecution?" (p. 144). Mary's leg-irons were put on only after Cranstoun's escape had prompted a petition to the King from "the Noblemen and Gentlemen in the Neighbourhood of Henley-upon-Thames", which in turn produced a letter from the Duke of Newcastle to the Sheriff, "requiring him to take more particular Care of her, as she stood charged with a Crime of so wicked a Nature, and black a Dye." (*Horrid Parricide*, p. 15).

Feelings about the crime itself were already running high, though. In a year which saw the passing of an Act to curb the alarming increase of murders (an Act under which convicted murderers could be immediately executed and then anatomized or hanged in chains), Mary Blandy's case attracted more public interest and attention than any other. The levels of interest were particularly high considering that it was not only a provincial murder but a provincial trial. Responses to the case were polarized and polarizing: clergymen and hacks, butterflies and bluestockings, demonstrated with equal vehemence just why Mary Blandy must be guilty, or must be innocent. Among the supporters of Blandy's innocence was the internationally renowned translator of Epictetus, Elizabeth Carter, whose friend Catherine Talbot (herself a poet and essayist) wrote to her on a warning note:

> I am sorry to hear you are so much concerned for that poor wretched creature Blandy, and think she has been too severely judged. I fear when the trial comes on you will find too full proof of guilt, and even hardiness in guilt that is shocking to think of . . . . On the whole her idea [i.e. the idea of her] is too terrible to dwell on.[9]

There were two factors which made the idea of Mary Blandy "too terrible to dwell on". The first, and less important, was class; the second, more basic, was the outraging of nature in the crime of parricide.

"Who could have thought that Miss *Blandy*, a young Lady virtuously brought up, distinguished for her good Behaviour and prudent Conduct in life . . . should ever be brought to a Tryal . . . for the most desperate and bloodiest kind of Murder . . . ?" asked Mr Serjeant Hayward, seconding Bathurst's opening speech for the Crown (*Tryal*, p. 9). Mary's virtuous and respectable education should have made her crime impossible, as the judge pointed out when passing sentence: "One should have thought, your own Sense [intelligence rather than common sense], your Education, and even the natural Softness of your Sex, might have secured you from an Attempt so barbarous and so wicked." (*Tryal*, p. 46). Instead, Mary's status and upbringing aggravated her guilt. The pamphlet which shows Mary drinking tea in gaol also reports that Mary had taken her own tea-chest with her when she was arrested, "as the Cannisters [*sic*] were all most full of fine Hyson, which she said would save her some Money" (*Horrid Parricide*, p. 13); and tea-drinking is one of the unsuitably genteel pursuits in which she indulges while awaiting trial:

> Her Behaviour in Gaol from the first has been very serene and calm; but she did not appear so deeply and sincerely affected as could be expected for one in her Circum-

stances, she always drinking Tea twice a Day, sometimes
walking in the Keeper's Garden with a Guard, and playing at Cards in the Evening; refusing to be seen by any
Persons, except her own particular Friends, who first sent
in their Names, and then but very few. (*Horrid Parricide*,
p. 15)

Miss Blandy, serenely exercising a gentlewoman's privi-
leges, including the right not to be at home to callers, breaches
one decorum by maintaining another. This pamphlet tells
elsewhere how, showing too much emotion this time instead
of too little, she had sworn at the servants after her father's
death, and remarks on "this strange Behaviour in Miss, so
unbecoming a Gentlewoman in her Circumstances" (p. 9).
There could be no "becoming" behaviour, though, for "a
Gentlewoman in her Circumstances"; no true gentlewoman
would find herself in those circumstances in the first place.
What was clear, however, was the spectacular unbecoming-
ness of Mary's behaviour as a daughter. Discussing Mary's
alleged attempt to escape from Mr Blandy's house while the
post-mortem was taking place, one writer asked: "What, but
a troubled Conscience, could prompt you to so strange and
indecent an Action, as the walking out of Town alone in a
high Road, while your Father lay dead?"[10] (Mary claimed
that she had been unable to bear the house while her father
was being "opened" in it, and that, in any case, as her garters
and shoe-buckles had been taken from her on Dr Addington's
orders, she was hardly dressed for escape.) Mary, the
prosecution said, had also failed to show grief, compassion or
remorse for her father's suffering and death; it was even
alleged that she had not only asked Betty Binfield, in the
middle of the night after Mr Blandy's death, to go to London
with her there and then, but that she had claimed to be "only
joking" when Betty refused:

> Only joking! good God! would she now have it thought
> she was only joking!
> Her Father just dead by Poison: She suspected of having
> poison'd him; accus'd of being a Parricide; and would

> she have it thought she was capable of joking? (*Tryal*,
> p. 8)

A woman capable of that, Bathurst suggests, is capable of
anything, even the hideous crime of parricide.

The particular heinousness of that crime is clear from
Hardwicke's decision to authorize a prosecution by, and at
the expense of, the Crown, when the more usual course would
have been a prosecution brought by the victim's family: "it
would be a Reproach to the King's Justice ... if such an
atrocious Crime of Poisoning & Parricide should escape
unpunished", he wrote to Newcastle, even going so far as to
suggest that Mary Blandy's crime might constitute "Petty
Treason". A woman convicted of petit treason could be burnt
at the stake, as Catherine Hayes had been in 1726 for killing
her husband.[11] Hardwicke's linking of "Poisoning & Parricide" offers a clue to the violence of reactions (his own
included) to the Blandy case. Mr Serjeant Hayward's opening
speech at Mary's trial made the same connection:

> Of all kinds of Murders, that by Poison is the most
> dreadful, as it takes a Man unguarded, and gives him
> no Opportunity to defend himself; much more so when
> administred [*sic*] by the Hand of a Child, whom one
> could least suspect, and from whom one might naturally
> look for Assistance and Comfort. (*Tryal*, p. 9)

The added horror of poisoning, for the male legal system,
is that the "Hand" offering food will almost always be female.
Poison is traditionally seen as a woman's weapon, and murder
by poison as the worst of crimes, a premeditated attack on a
defenceless victim. (Recent judicial treatments of women's
"premeditated" attacks on men, as somehow worse than
men's sudden, but no less fatal, attacks on women, come to
mind here.) The threat of murder within one's own family,
and, worse still (in an age when a middle-class "family" would
include servants), by one's own kin, was also raised by another
contemporary case: that of Elizabeth Jeffries (spelt variously
as Jeffries, Jeffreys or Jefferies), to whom Mary Blandy was
frequently compared. Miss Jeffries was convicted, with a ser-

vant, John Swan, of murdering her wealthy uncle, Mr Joseph Jeffries, a retired butcher at Walthamstow, who had adopted her at the age of five – and (people said) debauched her at the age of fifteen. "What a Shudder must humane Nature receive," the prosecution remarked,

> when it recollects there is no Place where Security may be depended upon, but at the same Time Persons are barring their Doors from Thieves without, they are inclosing worse Enemies within: Nay, the nearest Ties of Kindred are no Security. How amazing it is, that in this present polite Age, one single Year affords more Instances of the most unnatural Barbarity than a whole Age has done . . . .[12]

As a correspondent to *The Gentleman's Magazine* in March 1752 pointed out, despite the "exclamations . . . now made on female cruelty", there had been other murders "perpetrated this very year, which are no less shocking, tho' less talked of", among them the recent case of a father convicted, together with his common-law wife, of murdering "his own daughter by repeated acts of torture".[13] This case is mentioned once in *The London Magazine*, and not at all in *The Universal Magazine* or *The Covent-Garden Journal*, although all of these carried several lengthy articles on the Blandy trial. Even the letter-writer in *The Gentleman's Magazine*, after calling attention to this case, proceeds to the main purpose of his or her letter, which is "to send you more than a parallel to Miss *Blandy*'s case" – the story of a girl who killed her father with a hatchet, in his garden one snowy morning, and successfully framed her brother for the crime.[14]

The further horror of parricide lies in its inversion of the accepted power-structure – the betrayal of the creator by his creation, the destruction of "The Author of my Being, the very Fountain of my Life".[15] This betrayal of the father is equated with an offence against God the Father, as one of the attacks on Mary Blandy makes clear:

> Once, Miss, you had two Fathers to provide for and protect you; one by the Ties of Nature, the other by the

Bonds of Grace and Religion – And now! your earthly
Parent is your Accuser, and your heavenly One your
Judge. Both are become your Enemies. – Good God!
What deep Distress is this! where can Misery like this
find Comfort and Relief?[16]

The parallel between Mary's earthly and heavenly
Fathers recurs in many accounts of the case. As the judge's
remarks when sentencing Mary suggest, however, the character of Mary's earthly father made her offence even worse:

You are convicted of a Crime, so dreadful, so horrid in
itself that human Nature shudders at it. – *The wilful
Murder of your own Father!* – A Father, by all accounts, the
most fond, the most tender, the most indulgent that ever
lived: – That Father, with his dying Breath forgave you;
– May your heavenly Father do so too. (*Tryal*, pp. 45–6)

The prosecution made much of Mr Blandy's protective
love for Mary: Bathurst refers to her as "the Darling of [Mr
Blandy's] Soul, the Comfort of his Age" (*Tryal*, p. 4), while
Hayward calls her "his own, – his only, – his beloved Child",
and rather illogically exclaims: "O! were he now living, and
to see his Daughter there, the severest Tortures that Poison
could give, would be nothing to what he would suffer from
such a Sight." (*Tryal*, p. 9). According to Susannah Gunnell,
the dying Mr Blandy not only forgave Mary, but did his best
to shield her from prosecution:

... The Daughter said, Oh! Sir, your Tenderness
towards me is like a Sword to my Heart; every Word you
say is like Swords piercing my Heart, much worse, than
if you were to be ever so angry. I must down on my
Knees, and beg you will not curse me.
Council. What said the Father?
Gunnell. He said, *I curse thee! my Dear, how couldst thou think
I could curse thee? No I bless thee, and hope God will bless thee,
and amend thy Life*; and said further, *Do, my Dear, go out of
my Room, say no more, lest thou shouldst say any thing to thy
own Prejudice* ... (*Tryal*, p. 20)

In the hands of the prosecution, Mr Blandy's tenderness was not so much a sword to Mary's heart as a noose round her neck:

> She says she gave her Father this Powder to make him love her. – After having heard the great Affection with which the poor dying Man behaved towards her, can you think she wanted any Charm for that Purpose? After having heard what her own Witnesses have said of the Father's Fondness for the Daughter, can you believe she had Occasion for any Love-powder? (*Tryal*, p. 34)

Against the saintly figure of Mr Blandy, the prosecution pitted a monstrous daughter, who cursed her father for a rogue, a villain, and a toothless old dog, and who was heard to say: "*Who would grudge to send an old Father to Hell for 10,000 l.?*" (*Tryal*, p. 5). Mary was caught in a double bind: if she agreed with the prosecution's picture of her father, it destroyed the "love-powder" argument; if she tried to excuse her allegedly unfilial behaviour by pointing out Mr Blandy's bad temper and capriciousness, she strengthened the case against her as a daughter who needed to get her difficult father out of the way. "Sometimes little Family Affairs have happened," she pleaded at the trial, "and he did not speak to me so kind as I could wish. – I own I am passionate, My Lords, and in those Passions some hasty Expressions might have dropt . . . " (*Tryal*, p. 30). Mary's own *Account*, written after her conviction, showed the relationship in a different light, with herself (less passionate and hasty) trying to be a dutiful daughter to an increasingly harsh and volatile, but much loved, parent, who, having first favoured the match with Cranstoun, turned against him and even against his own daughter:

> The Morning [Cranstoun] left *Henley*, my Father parted with him with the greatest Tenderness; yet the Moment he was gone, he used me very cruelly on his Account. This had such an Effect upon me, that it threw me into Hysteric Fits. His Conduct for some Time was very uncertain; sometimes extremely tender, and at other

Times the reverse; he on certain Occasions saying very
bitter and cruel Things to me. (*Account*, p. 21)

While some contemporary versions of the story presented
Mary's criticisms of her father as yet another instance of her
wickedness, others repeated and embellished those criticisms
even when they did not agree with Mary's image of herself as
a model of filial piety.[17] Mr Blandy's character, crucial to the
prosecution's case, remains a puzzle for the reader. It is not
clear why he lied about Mary's marriage portion (far from
having £10,000 to spare, he was worth less than £4,000),
however Bathurst might describe that lie as "a pious Fraud"
(*Tryal*, p. 4). Why he continued to put up with Cranstoun for
so long is also a mystery, given his barrister brother-in-law's
obvious suspicion and hostility. Cranstoun's aristocratic connections must have been an attraction; and it may be, too,
that Cranstoun's story of a blackmailing, Catholic hussy
would have found more eager listeners in an England still
recovering from the shock of the '45. Assuming that Mr
Blandy was not taken in, however, he might still have found
Cranstoun's presence useful. Joan Morgan, in her novel about
Mary Blandy, *The Hanging Wood*, creates a believable picture
of Mr Blandy as an obsessive and possessive father, wanting
to show his daughter off to other men and yet keep her always
with him, encouraging Cranstoun's courtship because it could
never come to fruition.[18] Whether or not Mr Blandy really
thought Mary innocent, and tried to save her, remains uncertain, too, both in Gunnell's evidence and in Dr Addington's
account of his own conversation with the dying Mr Blandy:

I ask'd him, whom he suspected to be the Giver of the
Poison? The Tears stood in his Eyes, yet he forced a
Smile, and said; – – – *A poor Love-sick Girl* – – – *I forgive
her* – – – *I always thought there was Mischief in those cursed
Scotch Pebbles.* (*Tryal*, p. 13)

The image of the father made powerless by, and eventually falling victim to, his great love for his daughter, of
paternal power submerged in paternal tenderness, was one
exploited not only by the prosecution, but by the author of *The*

Fair Parricide, quick to recognize the emotional and dramatic potential of a love between father and daughter which proved fatal to both. "You too well know, *Maria*, the Power you hold o'er an indulgent Father", Blandford tells his daughter; and, confirming his prophetic fears, his death is a direct result of his "partial Love, indulgent to my Child" – not because his trust in Maria is misplaced, but because she does not realize Cranmore's unworthiness until it is too late and she has already poisoned her father by mistake.[19]

Blandford's deathbed follows the same emotional pattern as the legend of Mr Blandy's dying moments (without the intrusive narrating presence of Susannah Gunnell); Blandford rejects any suggestion that Maria is guilty, adding that such accusations "are far more bitter, give me severer Anguish than my approaching Fate" (p. 32). Maria, overwhelmed by his generosity, asks if he should not rather curse her and "blot this Parricide for ever from your Heart", adding that only her death "can suffice to expiate to the World even the Possibility of a Crime like Parricide". He urges her to beware of incriminating herself in "this wild Extravagance of frantic Grief", and to avoid "the enticing Wiles of Love's pernicious Lure", after which he dies in giving her his blessing: "Oh! I have yet a thousand tender Things, my Child; but they are lost in misty Darkness – Bless – – – Bless her Heaven! Farewel! O farewel! my dear *Maria*." (pp. 33–4).

The rest of the play is rather an anticlimax after this apotheosis of the father. Mary Blandy's own death, however, recalled the heroism of her father's last moments, and restored to her much of the public sympathy she had lost, as Horace Walpole waspishly noted: "Miss Blandy died with a coolness of courage that is astonishing, and denying the fact, which has made a kind of party in her favour; as if a woman who would not stick at parricide, would scruple a lie!"[20] At the other extreme of the emotional register from the solemnity of the judge or the grave concern of the clergymen, Walpole and his friends found the Blandy and Jeffries cases entertaining as well as shocking. "Since the two Misses [Blandy and Jefferies] were hanged, and the two Misses [the Gunnings] were married, there is nothing at all talked of", Walpole quotes Lady Gower as saying (*Letters*, vol. II, p. 290).

The Gunning sisters provide an interesting counterpart to Blandy and Jeffries, those sisters in crime. Beautiful but penniless, these Irish girls had taken London by storm in 1751. Wherever they went, they would be so mobbed by enthusiastic crowds that they had to go home again. (Mary Blandy, making her alleged escape attempt on the day of the post-mortem, was so surrounded by an angry mob that she had to be escorted in a closed carriage for the quarter of a mile to home.) Clever parental management, and the fact that the beautiful sisters were always seen together, brought the Gunnings extraordinary success in the London marriage-market: Maria became Countess of Coventry; while Elizabeth's scandalous marriage to the Duke of Hamilton was performed at midnight, with a curtain-ring, at the house of the famous marriage-broker, Mr Keith, but was no less binding a marriage for all that. When she was presented at Court after the honeymoon, people climbed on chairs to catch a glimpse of her.[21] Walpole's first mention of Mary Blandy, in March 1752, occurs just after a passage on these celebrated sisters:

> The world is still mad about the Gunnings . . . . There are mobs at their doors to see them get into their chairs; and people go early to get places at the theatre when it is known they will be there . . . . There are two wretched women that just now are as much talked of, a Miss Jefferies and a Miss Blandy; the one condemned for murdering her uncle, the other her father. Both their stories have horrid circumstances; the first, having been debauched by her uncle; the other had so tender a parent, that his whole concern while he was expiring, and knew her for his murderess, was to save her life. (*Letters*, vol. II, p. 281)

The Gunning sisters' success must have been the envy and the ideal of many young women and their ambitious parents. It also prompted a cautionary tale by Dr William Dodd, *The Sisters*, published in 1754, which showed the sad fate of two beautiful sisters who dream of going to London and coming back with coronets on their coaches. One sister, Caroline, survives her trials and tribulations and makes a

respectable marriage; the other, Lucy, succumbs early to
seduction, sinks into prostitution, and is so brutally attacked
by clients that she dies, though not before she has had an
affecting reunion with the father who so unwisely encouraged
his daughter's matrimonial ambitions.[22]

What Mary Blandy and Elizabeth Jeffries had in common
with the Gunnings was their status as spectacle, their ability
to draw crowds. As the equation of Misses hanged and Misses
married suggests, though, spectacular – even spectacular in
success – is not really the right thing for a woman to be. Mary
Blandy, going to execution, was only too well aware of the
spectacle she presented, and of the thin line between being
spectacular and making a spectacle of oneself. Dressed
"extremely neat", her arms and hands bound with "black
paduasoy ribbons", Mary Blandy prayed fervently with the
Revd Mr Swinton before making her final declaration of innocence to the crowd which had gathered to see her hanged:

> As she ascended the ladder, she said, *Gentlemen, don't hang
> me high for the sake of decency*; and then being desired to
> step up a little higher, she did two steps, and turning
> herself about, she trembled, and said, *I am afraid I shall
> fall*. After this the halter was put about her neck, and
> she pull'd down her handkerchief over her face, without
> shedding one tear all the time.[23]

Mary Blandy's stoicism in the face of her own death made
her a heroine as surely as her failure to mourn satisfactorily for
her father had made her a monster. Her concern for "decency"
even in her last moments has seemed rather comical to modern
commentators, perhaps forgetting that this was an era when
women's basic undergarment was a shift; when the gallows
was high, and hanging itself a protracted and clumsy process
of strangulation, in which a body might "dance upon the
rope" for half an hour or so; and that therefore not only legs
but genitals might be exposed. Mary Blandy's attempt to
protect her body from further violation in death was, in any
case, unsuccessful: "In about half an hour the body was cut
down, and carried thro' the croud upon the shoulders of a
man with her legs exposed very indecently, for two or three

hundred yards, to a neighbouring house, where it was put
into a coffin, and from thence conducted to *Henley . . . .*"[24]

Even though she escaped being anatomized, Mary was
indecently exposed after death. The story which had begun
so genteelly at Paradise, Lord Mark Ker's house in Henley,
had made many such indecent exposures, showing the intimate details of the Blandys' family life: Mr Blandy being
shaved in the kitchen; servants eating and drinking leftovers
out of their master's and mistresses' dishes; stale gruel being
warmed up yet again for an invalid's supper; cold tea poured
into the cat's basin and spurned by the cat; Mr Blandy vomit-
ing in the night. Mr Blandy's body, too, had been intimately
examined, and at last cut open, its secrets displayed and
described for the interested public. Mary herself had struggled
for a long time to hold on to "decency", not in the sense of
decorum, or concern for her audience's sensibilities, but in an
attempt to keep intact the dignity of her own body. Confined
to her room with a man guarding her day and night; refused
"a Maid for the common Decencies of my Sex" (*Tryal*, p. 30);
forbidden to listen at her father's door when he was dying;
her clothes, letters, and keys taken from her; her letter to
Cranstoun broken open and read in court; her private life
bandied about in libellous pamphlets, and her legs swollen
from the irons, Mary had suffered repeated violations of her
privacy and her dignity. Her attempts to retain that dignity,
whether in her ladylike ways in gaol, or in her protests in
court about the many humiliations she had suffered, merely
told against her the more. Having failed to satisfy filial decorum, Mary Blandy could not now appeal to her status as a
gentleman's daughter.

The stories told by and about Mary Blandy brought
together different forms and different audiences: solemn and
satirical; high and low; official and intimate. In addition to
all the contradictory accounts of what really happened, the
case of Mary Blandy yoked together disparate and incongru-
ous elements: the English marriage-market and the Scottish
marriage laws; the events of the '45 and the fashions in
women's jewellery; the daughter of a provincial attorney and
the son of a Scots peer; the lady and the gruel-pan; love-
powder and deadly poison; a dying father's forgiveness putting

a noose round his daughter's neck; a no longer private gentlewoman suffering a véry public death.

"Guilty, or guiltless, who can surely tell;/A spotless Angel, or a Fiend of Hell?", shrugs the Prologue to *The Fair Parricide*. A three-act tragedy is an obvious form of fictionalization, but there were many other, more subtle, fictionalizations of the Blandy case. The subject lent itself all the more readily to such treatment, because the father–daughter bond was, throughout the century, a staple of fiction. Mary Blandy's story fits into an available pattern of father–daughter relationships, with a set repertoire of events, gestures, and rhetoric – tears, kneeling, blessings, curses, solemn oaths, apostrophes to heaven, threats, prohibitions, pleas for forgiveness, deathbed reconciliations, and so on.[25] The language used in many of these scenes, as it comes down to us, seems at times formulaic, ready-made, whether because in moments of stress life imitated art, or because the rhetorical conventions of reporting were so strong. "Exactly them words", says Betty Binfield with satisfaction, retailing Mary Blandy's suspiciously theatrical remark, *"Who would grudge to send an old Father to Hell for 10,000 l?"*[26] It is, after all, what Mr Blandy's monstrous daughter ought to have said.

The character roles, too, often seem pre-set: Susannah Gunnell, the brave and faithful old retainer; Dr Addington, the expert taking charge, the mainspring of the prosecution; Mrs Blandy, the foolishly encouraging mother; Mr Serjeant Stevens, the warning voice going unheard; Cranstoun, the younger son, roving soldier and opportunist; and the two central characters, whose ambivalence makes the drama possible. Was Mr Blandy a loving father or a manipulative tyrant? Was Mary an innocent dupe or a vicious schemer, a "poor Love-sick Girl" or an embittered old maid?

Mary Blandy becomes the heroine, or anti-heroine, in a constantly reworked story which many people tell themselves in different ways and for different reasons. To Horace Walpole and friends, she offers a tale to fill an idle hour, before returning to the latest (preferably scandalous) novel. To Elizabeth Carter and Catherine Talbot, she prompts a far more serious and sombre psychological study. For the unknown author of *The Fair Parricide*, her story provides an ideal dramatic situation, replete with shocking discoveries and agonizing remorse. For the lawyers and clerics, she becomes an Awful Warning, showing "the dreadful Consequence of Disobedience to a Parent" (*Tryal*, p. 9), of unbridled lust, or of the modern young woman's Godless education, "falsely called LIBERAL" (*Account*, p. 52). The ease with which Mary's crime could be written and rewritten gives the lie to contemporary writers' repeated insistence on its monstrous and unimaginable nature. If "Poisoning & Parricide" struck at the conventions of filial piety and decorum, Mary Blandy's story, in all its many versions, restored the comfortingly familiar structures of everyday life – and everyday fiction.

Celebration and Exorcism:
The Daughter–Mother Relation in the
Fiction of Alice Munro

Flora Alexander

Despite the centrality in women's lives of the relationship between daughter and mother, literary treatments of this subject, especially before the twentieth century, have been limited in range. In the fiction of the nineteenth century, it is the *absence* of mothers (e.g. those of Emma Woodhouse, Jane Eyre, and Isabel Archer) which is striking; clearly the lack of a mother who might provide emotional security or a restraining influence allows fruitful opportunities for plot development. Where a mother does exist in nineteenth-century novels she is frequently constructed, like Mrs Bennett or Mrs Tulliver, as a foil for a more brilliant daughter. Marianne Hirsch, examining developments in the treatment of the relationship as a literary subject, has commented that there is in European and American literature of the nineteenth century, and also in modernist and post-modernist plots, a "desire for the heroine's singularity based on a disidentification from the fate of other women, especially mothers."[1]

Adrienne Rich sees the cathexis, or concentration of psychic energy, between mother and daughter as "the great unwritten story", and she puts forward a number of possible reasons why it has been neglected in writing and in art.[2] She suggests that mother-and-daughter relationships have been partly obscured by concentration on the powerful dyad of mother and son, and she also argues that for men, the mother–

daughter relationship, like relationships between women generally, has been perceived as threatening. She also points out that tensions may exist between a woman artist and her mother, who is likely to be a more traditional and family-centred woman, and proposes that this may have inhibited the portrayal of mother figures by writer-daughters. During the twentieth century many of the conditions in which women write have changed, and women writers have added considerably to the literature of motherhood. The relationship between a woman and her mother is charged with powerful emotions, and texts based on a daughter's position with regard to a mother figure draw on materials such as the resolution of tensions between the two women, the acceptance of each other's imperfections, the daughter's search for freedom from restrictions placed on her behaviour, and her progress to emergence as a separate individual.

Alice Munro has made a significant contribution to fictional portrayals of the daughter–mother relationship. She has published, between 1968 and 1990, seven volumes of short stories, many of which contain some consideration of daughters and their mothers. Sometimes a story is constructed so that the perspective and the time-scale shift, and a figure who was initially presented as a mother is eventually seen also as a daughter, as in "The Progress of Love", in which the behaviour of the narrator's mother is slowly revealed to be the result of her own childhood experience.[3] The emphasis here seems to be on the inexorability of parental influences, which are of course not exclusively the preserve of women, but which interest Munro particularly as they pass through generations in the female line. But the most obviously recurring interest in her treatment of motherhood is in the examination of how a daughter's life is affected by aspects of her interaction with her mother. Two of the books, *Lives of Girls and Women* (1971) and *The Beggar Maid: Stories of Flo and Rose* (first published in 1978 under the title *Who Do You Think You Are?*), consist of stories linked to form a study of the development of a female subject, and in both of these the interaction between the young woman and a mother figure is central.[4] In *Lives of Girls and Women* Del's mother exerts on her an influence which is partly valued and partly resisted. Flo in *The Beggar*

Maid is actually Rose's stepmother, but at the same time the only mother Rose has known. The two emerge as very different people, but the contribution made by Flo to Rose's life plays an essential part in her development to womanhood.

Lives of Girls and Women is a text produced at a time when feminist activity was stimulating an extensive scrutiny and revision of ideas about femininity, and the text reflects a widening awareness of different patterns of life which women may adopt.[5] Through the sustained exploration of Del's formation it examines and challenges different views of women's roles and capacities. The girl is placed in the context of the influences of mother, father, and other members of their family, and also of other models of behaviour available in a small Canadian country town. The traditional paradigm according to which an adventurous female hero asserts her individuality and right to freedom, against pressures from a conventional mother, is varied in this text. Del's mother, Ada or Addie, is not a conventional woman: she is committed to new ways of thinking, and eager to explain her advanced outlook to Del and to anyone else who will listen, so that she is seen as a "wild-woman", and creates embarrassment for her teenage daughter (p. 64). As a result, Del's progress to maturity is rendered complex. She must define herself as different from her mother, while at the same time preserving her freedom from the limitations of conventional feminine roles.

Addie's deviance from the normal attitudes and behaviour of the women in a small country town is clarified by the contrasting figures of her husband's unmarried aunts, who, for example, find fault with her careless attitude to domestic skills. In turn they, and the rest of their family, possess attitudes which Addie finds negative: to them, refusing an opportunity for advancement is acceptable, even admirable, while to her progressive mind the "beauties of the negative" are incomprehensible (p. 38). Further, Del explains their different ways of thinking in terminology that resembles many analyses of feminine as opposed to (male) logocentric thought processes: "My mother went along straight lines, Aunt Elspeth and Auntie Grace wove in and out around her, retreating and disappearing and coming back, slippery and soft-voiced and indestructible" (p. 36).[6] Del appreciates their fluid, indirect qualities in a way that her mother cannot: "She pushed them out of her way as if they were cobwebs; I knew better than that" (p. 37). Addie's characteristics are defined further by the difference between her and her lodger, Fern Dogherty. Fern is displayed as a type of a sexual, self-indulgent femininity, her softness and ripeness contrasting with Addie's "sharpness, smartness, determination, selectiveness" (p. 141).

As Del moves through adolescence her need to find a satisfactory concept of femininity becomes acute. Watching her friend Naomi adapt to a norm of graceless courtship and elaborate plans for home-making, and finally become trapped by pregnancy into a marriage for which she has little enthusiasm, she formulates for herself the question, "What was a normal life?" (p. 191). At the same time that she feels alienated from this standard pattern of behaviour for young women in Jubilee, Ontario, she is also deeply disturbed by stereotyped theories of femininity which reach her through argument with boys at school. She resists frantically the sexist account of male and female patterns of thought she finds in a magazine article by a Freudian psychiatrist from New York.[7] She feels a pressure to conform to general expectations of femininity, because she wants men to love her, but at the same time she wants to be free to think in a way that is abstract and not personal (p. 178). Her mother should be for her a source of support in resisting essentialist theories about women's intellectual capacities. She knows that her mother's response will be "Oh, it is just that maddening male nonsense, women have no brains." Yet she holds back from identification with her mother's views: she does not want to be like her mother, with her "virginal brusqueness, her innocence". And indeed Addie's feminist view as presented in the text is over-simple. The author has said of her speech which provides the title of the work,

> There is a change coming I think in the lives of girls and women. . . . All women have had up till now has been their connection with men. . . . Once you make that mistake, of being – distracted, over a man, your life will never be your own. (p. 173)

that she intended it to be ironic because, while she feels affection for the character, she meant to create her as a woman whose analysis of issues does not take adequate account of their complexity.[8] Del has to find her own way which recognizes the value in her mother's stance, but avoids the weaknesses in it: "I myself was not so different from my mother, but concealed it, knowing what dangers there were" (p. 80).

Del's sexual development becomes the focal point for the tension between mother and daughter. In her childhood she has sensed an inadequacy in her mother's brisk attitude to relationships, as when she is unable to speak of love as her reason for marrying Del's father, and confines herself to saying that he was "always a gentleman" (p. 78). Later the issue is more specifically focused on sex. Addie sees sex as something that no intelligent woman would submit to unless she had to (p. 199). When Del, sexually attracted to Garnet French, is overwhelmed by the unsuspected pleasures the relationship brings her, her mother sees her as "addled over a boy", in a way that intelligence should protect her from (p. 217). The daughter's compulsion to follow a path different from her mother's is defined graphically by Del's response to the loss of her virginity, which takes place unceremoniously while she leans against the wall of her mother's house. The next day in a gesture of combined evasion and assertion she draws her mother's attention to the trace of her blood which the event has left on the path, inventing an explanation that it was deposited there by a tom-cat killing a bird (p. 224). The text treats the conflict between daughter and mother in an open way. On the one hand, the limitations of Addie's puritanism are clearly displayed. Yet Del eventually recognizes that her affair with Garnet has been "play", and the narrative shows that in the course of it she was risking pregnancy and the consequent loss of freedom in the same way that her friend Naomi did (p. 234). Her emergence from the affair is a source of pain, but she also sees it as an awakening, and her mother's position is at least partly vindicated (p. 237).

The Beggar Maid resembles *Lives of Girls and Women* in that it traces the development of a gifted young woman growing up in the restricted society of a small town in Ontario. Rose's experience is different from Del's, in that she is brought up by a stepmother, Flo, who married her father after Rose's mother died. Del's task of finding for herself a subjectivity separate from that of her mother therefore does not arise in the same way for Rose, who has no difficulty in seeing herself as different from Flo. The relationship between the two is largely one of contrast between the practical, limited Flo and the reflective and imaginative Rose. Yet Rose's sense of separateness is to some extent questioned. She has imagined recollections of the time when she was a baby and her mother was alive as a "far gentler and more ceremonious time", but the text makes clear that this is based only on the survival from that time of some patterned egg-cups, and also that Rose has effectively "known only Flo for a mother" (p. 4). This is recognized not only by the narrator but also eventually by Rose herself. Before her marriage into a rich West Coast family, she brings her fiancé, Patrick, on an uneasy visit to meet Flo, and he assumes that her real parents must have been different from Flo in her limitation and vulgarity. Rose, despite her discomfort with Flo's way of life, has a sense of loyalty that makes her dissent from his desire to provide her with a more elegant real family. Her attitude to Flo and her upbringing remains contradictory. Even in middle age, when she contemplates the gulf between her attitudes and Flo's, she recognizes that most of her friends experience a similar gulf between themselves and the "disappointed" homes they came from (p. 190). And she continues to perceive Flo's house, long after the death of her father, as "home" (p. 183).

Rose's progress towards self-definition, like Del's, is a matter of finding a balance between intellect and emotion. The task is more obvious and straightforward for her than it is for Del, who has to negotiate a complex position in relation to her mother's attitudes. For Rose the primary difficulty lies in her father's desire to believe that women should be practical and not intellectual (p. 47). Flo is hostile to books, whereas Rose is ambitious and enjoys academic work; "her whole life was in her head" (p. 48). Rose's father is torn between pride in his daughter and a desire to please Flo, who is his idea of what a woman ought to be. Rose resists the pressure to conform to a limited stereotype of how women should think and behave, with a sense of unease, but with the same determination that makes her later disregard the sterile academicism of the lecturer Dr Henshawe, who thinks that because she is "a scholar" she should keep herself aloof from college social life and sexual liaisons (p. 72).

Despite the polarization between Flo's anti-intellectualism and Rose's life of the mind, the two engage in a female activity of shared story-telling signalled in the sub-title, "Stories of Flo and Rose". Flo listens while Rose tells stories of sexual activity which her father would disapprove of (p. 43). Flo tells tales which fall outside the everyday happenings of the town. She has some acquaintance with a wider world, having once worked as a waitress in Toronto's Union Station. Characteristically, her narrative offerings concern the horrors and grotesqueries of life: she has a repertoire of tales of violence, incest, and suicide. Much of the story-telling in *The Beggar Maid* is there either to draw attention to the "Gothic" quality of ordinary experience, or else to be a vehicle for Alice Munro's continuing preoccupation with the whole nature of the enterprise of fiction and metafiction. But occasionally the stories coalesce to make, additionally, a point about the lives of women. The story "Half a Grapefruit" brings together in a highly productive conjunction several strands of narrative in which women are oppressed and incur varieties of disgrace. Rose is aware of her father's desire for women to be practical, but intellectually naïve: her choice of a life of the mind amounts to a kind of "disgrace" (p. 47). This idea is placed alongside an account of a more obvious kind of scandal, in which Ruby Carruthers incurs general contempt for her sexual promiscuity, while her male partners escape all censure. There is a further anecdote, told by Rose, of an entirely disproportionate scandal, occasioned by a girl's accidentally dropping a sanitary towel at school, thus provoking the Principal to vow publicly to "discover, expose, flog, and expel the culprit who had put it on view" (p. 42). The effect of bringing together three such diverse cases of misogynist attitudes is to create a comprehensive sense of a society that oppresses women.

The death of the mother is a topic which recurs in Alice

Munro's fiction, in texts produced over a period of thirty years from 1960 to 1990. For a woman the death of her mother creates a challenging situation, which has inevitable effects on her subjectivity. Issues of loss, grief, and guilt are associated with the experience, together with the need to recognize the fact of separation. Munro has referred in an interview to the basis for her continuing interest in the topic of the paralysed and dying mother, in that her own mother became ill with Parkinson's disease when she was quite young. Munro mentions in connection with this situation "The Peace of Utrecht", and also "The Ottawa Valley", which she describes as autobiographical.[9] Since that interview she has reworked some of the same material in the title story of *Friend of My Youth*.[10]

In "The Peace of Utrecht" the mother is not presented in detail as an individual: rather she is the figure of the sufferer from the Shaking Palsy, who weeps and struggles as she confronts her disease with what her daughter sees as "egotism feeding stubbornly even on disaster" (p. 199). The only sign of her personality is her desire to defy death by having brightly coloured clothes made for her. She is taken over by the bizarre nature of her illness, and thus inflicts humiliation on the daughters. They deal with the situation by treating her in a depersonalized way. Their phrase "our Gothic Mother" carries, among other things, the significance that she has ceased to be the individual she once was (p. 200). It is only the sister who went away who thinks that she can recollect something of what the mother had been. For the sister who stayed, the woman was destroyed by the disease. She is demanding as a child would be, and the daughters respond by cheating her of the emotion she desires, and with "parodies of love" (p. 199).

The story is told by Helen, the younger daughter who married and went away, leaving her older sister Maddy to look after their mother. The narrative presents her perspective during her return, with her children, to the family home in Jubilee, Ontario in the summer after the mother's death. The division into two parts is used dynamically to reflect process within the narrative. The first part reveals that Helen did not come home for her mother's funeral, and that she has not seen her mother for a number of years (p. 202). There are indications of her unease about the mother's illness and death.

As she enters the family home she allows herself in memory to hear the undisguised cry for help that she had shut out while the mother was alive (p. 198). She draws back from imagining the death: "She must have wept and struggled in that house of stone (as I can, but will not, imagine) until the very end." (p. 199).

In the second section, narrated slightly later, this is subjected to a savage irony. One of Helen's two old aunts reveals to her the circumstances of her mother's death, which she has shrunk from contemplating: that the mother did not struggle to the end *in her house*, because Maddy had put her in hospital, against her will; that the mother had tried, in spite of her paralysis, to run away; and that thereafter she had been confined with a board nailed across her bed (pp. 207–8). A key phrase used by Maddy, "No exorcising", which both opens and closes the first part of the story, has multiple significance (pp. 191, 202). Initially it appears to mean that the sisters should not dwell on their shared experience of abnormality and disaster. Later it takes on a further meaning, when it becomes apparent that Maddy, like Helen, carries a sense of guilt. Despite all that she did for the mother, Maddy feels the weight of the aunts' censure, conveyed in the remark made by Aunt Annie at the funeral, "May it never happen like that to you." (p. 208). "No exorcising" has a further ironic layer of meaning: it refers not only to Maddy's wish that they should avoid dwelling on the past, but also to the fact that neither daughter is in fact *capable* of exorcising the burden of guilt. Helen reflects that perhaps the last function of old women is "making sure the haunts [hauntings] we have contracted for are with us" (p. 209). And Maddy, despite wishing to take possession of her own life, finds herself unable to do so, even after her mother has died (p. 210).

The text is filled with perceptions of negativity. Helen had seen in the sick mother a threat to her own personal identity (p. 194). Yet after the mother's death her bleakness is not alleviated. Adversity has not strengthened the relationship between the sisters: they have not truly shared it, and they are now separated by a "desert" (p. 190). Helen does not understand why Maddy stayed (p. 196). Maddy remarks that no one except her lover Fred Powell speaks the same language

as she does (pp. 194, 209). The sisters' inability to communi-
cate is contrasted with the polished relationship, a "web of
sisterhood", of their elderly aunts (p. 203). Helen's identity
as a young mother is important to her, but the comfort of her
reflection that her children are fortunate and safe is undercut
by the further thought that this "may be what most parents
think at one time or another" (p. 201).

"The Ottawa Valley" is focused principally on the narrator's memories of a childhood visit to her mother's original
home in that area. A sense of the mother's individuality is
disclosed in this text through the daughter's recognition that
her mother is a more complex person than she had thought.
In spite of being a refined woman, she has a rapport with
more coarsely spoken relatives, and enjoys the recollection of
a practical joke in which she and a cousin once stitched up
the flies of a young man's overalls. The accumulation of small
details of the mother's behaviour on the visit, and the depiction of her relationships with other members of her family,
are sufficient to produce a powerful sense of what the daughter
has lost as a result of her death. As in "The Peace of Utrecht",
the burden caused by a mother's illness, and the daughter's
resentment of it, are made clearly apparent:

> after I had received the medical explanations of what was
> happening, I still felt secretly that she had given her
> consent. . . . For her own purposes, I felt she did it: dis-
> play, of a sort; revenge of a sort as well. (p. 233)

Aunt Dodie, actually the mother's cousin, tells her the harsh
news that her mother is ill, and will need to be looked after,
just as Dodie herself had as a girl looked after a sick mother.
This scene is reminiscent of the aunt's harrowing revelation
in the earlier story.

There is also a specific discussion of the effect produced
by the mother on the subjectivity of the daughter. In a meta-
fictional coda which echoes the failure to achieve exorcism in
"The Peace of Utrecht", the narrator deals explicitly with the
need to treat adequately the memory of the mother, remarking
that it is easier for her to see the other characters clearly:

And she is of course the one that I am trying to get; it is to reach her that this whole journey has been undertaken. With what purpose? To mark her off, to describe, to illumine, to celebrate, to *get rid*, of her; and it did not work, for she looms too close, just as she always did. (p. 233)

Added to this inability to escape, there is the narrator's awareness of her own likeness to her mother, which prevents her from ever truly gaining separation. She thinks of her mother in several different circumstances, and "more and more often lately when I look in the mirror" (p. 218). Comments made during the visit about family resemblances, such as "I see your own mother in this one", intensify the sense that individuals are taken over by a general family pattern (p. 231).

"Friend of My Youth" is in part a reworking of materials used in "The Ottawa Valley". As in the earlier story, the narrator's desire to come to terms with the death of her mother is made explicit, both at the beginning and at the end of the narrative. The recurrent concern to explore this theme is interwoven with new material: the story of the strictly fundamentalist Christian Flora, who accepts stoically the double loss of her prospects of marriage, first when her fiancé impregnates and marries her younger sister Ellie, and later when he marries the nurse who cared for the sister in her terminal illness. Structurally this story is characteristic of Munro's mature work in that it highlights the activity of story-telling, and in effect the dying mother material, reduced to the essential elements of her youth and marriage and her subsequent sickness and death, becomes a framework within which three different versions of the story of Flora are told. The key elements of the mother story are exposed by the spareness of the narration: the depersonalization of illness is made explicit. When the narrator dreams of her mother:

"I recovered then what in waking life I had lost – my mother's liveliness of face and voice before her throat muscles stiffened and a woeful, impersonal mask fastened itself over her features." (pp. 3–4)

A dream motif, first employed in "The Peace of Utrecht" (p. 200), is more fully developed here. In the early story it takes the form of a simple reference to dreams in which the daughter sees her mother, after her death, and perceives the illness as being much milder than she had remembered. In "Friend of My Youth" the idea is essentially the same, but the expanded treatment emphasizes the qualities, "the lightness and impatience and confidence" destroyed by the disease, and clarifies the complex state of mind of the dreamer. The dream allows her to achieve reconciliation and to get rid of guilt: "the strangest, kindest thing of all to me was her matter-of-fact reply. Oh well, she said, better late than never, I was sure I'd see you someday" (p. 4). Inevitably, because it is "too transparent . . . too easy . . . " (p. 3), the dream stops, and the narrator is left with the "bugbear" of her loss. The psychological complexities are recognized: the narrator feels also in a strange way cheated by the loss, when she has the happy dream, of the "bitter lump of love" to which she had grown attached (p. 26).

In both this story and "The Ottawa Valley" Alice Munro uses as an oblique parallel to the suffering mother the figure of a woman whose life is blighted not by disease but by the loss of her prospect of marriage. Aunt Dodie has a "tragic life", having been jilted on her wedding day; in "Friend of My Youth" Flora bears with equal stoicism her double betrayal. Both stories also contain motifs of the wedding dress, and repeated pregnancy (in Ellie's case doomed to recurrent miscarriage), which appear to function as tokens of the central importance for a woman of the married state that Dodie and Flora are denied. Their demeanour contrasts with the mother's appeal for love and pity, her undignified "stricken shadow" (p. 24). The figure of Flora is also used to define a crucial distinction between the natures of the narrator and her mother. Both think of making up a story about her, which would be different from the supposedly factual account which the daughter obtained from her mother and passes on to the reader. While the mother imaginatively sees Flora as "white", to the daughter she is "black". She expands on this: "What made Flora evil in my story was just what made her admirable in my mother's – her turning away from sex" (p. 22).

The mother views sex as "a dark undertaking", and it is perhaps significant that her marriage is recounted in terms of wedding dress, trousseau, gifts, with no mention at all of her husband. The narrator, by contrast, declares herself to be full of desire for male passion and domination. She notices what is lacking in her mother's factual account of the Grieveses' household: "my mother never reports anything that Robert said. . . . He must have been there" (p. 12). To her the really mysterious person, who captures her imagination, is Robert, and she creates for herself a romantic image of him, with a "sombre, shackled beauty" (p. 12). In spite of its apparently rambling structure, this most recent treatment of the dead mother theme is the most penetrating in its emphasis on the difference between the daughter and her mother, and the dissection of the daughter's complex feelings – her awareness of her own inadequacy, and her need for release from a painful burden, combined with the contrary element in her nature that clings to the "bitter lump of love".

In all of these stories, Alice Munro selects and combines essentially unremarkable events and emotions so that their conjunction is powerfully productive. She considers polarities between the small town and a more sophisticated, wider world, and the different effects of social change on older and younger women. In the context which is thus created, women's lives are examined with delicate perceptiveness and deep understanding. The meanings that emerge from the stories illuminate the contradictory forces which govern the relationship a daughter has with her mother, and demonstrate the arduousness and complexity of the process of separation which daughters must undergo.

Men Creating

Making Myths and *The Merchant's Tale*

Valerie Allen

Engels, in *The Origins of the Family*, contrasts the monogamous marriage as female domestic slavery with sex love that is freed from economic institutionalization.[1] In this sense, monogamy means strictly and exclusively the maintainance of patriarchal control of property through the line of male descent. Such a system of control can only be supported by curtailing women's sexual activity to ensure that the children they bear will be legitimate. Although what Engels refers to as modern individual sex love has become ideally (and falsely) identified with the monogamous marriage, its historical début, he remarks, can be seen in mediaeval courtly love which, as we all know from Lancelot and Guinevere, occurs outside the conjugal bed. In many ways courtly love, which makes the lady an all-powerful mistress and the lover a vassal-servant, inverts and feminizes the very economic system that uses monogamy for its ascendancy. For Engels, prostitution is simply monogamy's Other – the exposed economic underbelly twitching without its shell of domestic privilege. And by the same logic, mediaeval courtly love finds its distorted Other in the fabliau[2] – comic, obscene and materialized where romance is tragic, decorous and spiritualized. Romances tell stories about courtly virgins and fabliaux about town whores. If both courtly love and the fabliau can be read as an eroticized affirmation of feudal ties, they might also be read as the precursor of an emergent subjectivity that sets the individual's private sexual passion against the social and public contract of marriage. Courtly love and the fabliau effect a valorization of the feudal world and simultaneously chart its eclipse.

It is on this double-edged note that I wish to open my discussion of one of Geoffrey Chaucer's poems, *The Merchant's Tale*,[3] and I follow this introduction with a descriptive summary. It relates a patriarchal narrative that sounds depressingly familiar but also, by addressing the feminist reader from an historical point that so predates the rise of liberalism, it uncovers differences that pose fundamental questions about gendered identity and autonomy. The ontological and gendered oppositions that underpin the tale's accounts of linguistic, biological and artistic production are based on a relation of privation, of possession and lack. Contemporary feminisms – from Marxist to liberal – tend to base such oppositions on an ideal political relation of equality, and from this position it is justifiably hard not to view the female lot in the Middle Ages as nasty and brutish. By the same token, modern critics such as E.T. Donaldson and Charles Owen have invented the myth of the ironic Chaucer as a way of dissociating the father of English poesy from the unpalatable antifeminism of his writing. But if mediaevalism tyrannizes through a hierarchy of possession and lack, it also opens up the possibility of a dialectically related difference, of deconstructing the absolutism of essentialism yet retaining specific identity.

Fabliaux invariably commercialize sexual relations and Chaucer doubly underlines the vulgar economism of this one by narrating it through the Merchant, one of the Canterbury pilgrims. The tale is offered as a corroboration of the Merchant's personal experience of women as shrews and the complete idiocy of any man who marries one. It is an antifeminist *exemplum*. So before we even begin the story we already know its meaning or *sentence*, as Chaucer would put it. Thus the truth about women is seen to exist prior to its linguistic and material articulation.

The story divides traditionally into three parts. In the first (IV 1245–1688) we meet the main character, a doddering old knight called January who suddenly decides to marry. After a lengthily ironic apologia for marriage, the narrator describes January's debate with Justinus and Placebo. Placebo, by name and nature, simply echoes January's wishes but Justinus predicts the likelihood of conjugal strife. January is deaf to such advice and plumps for May, a pretty but low-born wench from the town. This first section is generally thought to be a comic reworking of Eustache Deschamps's contemporary *Miroir de Mariage*, an allegory of the salvation of the soul through free will's rejection of bodily appetite. Deschamps's central character, Franc Vouloir, an old man, rejects the demands of sensual appetite (his false counsellors) to marry, and submits to the demands of reason (his misogynist counsellor, Repertoire de Science). Against this background, the moral significance of Chaucer's tale becomes clearer. January dithers between his reason and his lower member and where Franc Vouloir chooses the former, January indulges the other one.

The second part (IV 1689–2020) relates the nuptials of January and May and the advent of Damien the lusty squire who completes the *ménage-à-trois*. January takes May to the marital bed – we are given a singularly offputting account of his fumblings and May's growing disaffection. Meanwhile, the love-lorn Damien slips a billet-doux to May who furtively reads it in the privy. On May's return, January overcomes his impotence and instructs her to pay her marriage debt. The ordeal finally persuades May to accept Damien as prospective lover.

The third part (IV 2021–2418) is a parody of the Fall – an aetiological fable that accounts for the total depravity of woman. January builds an enclosed garden, a *hortus conclusus*, an earthly Paradise with a small gate for which he alone keeps the key. The implicit uterine imagery is clear here. It is such a beautiful garden that even the king and queen of the underworld, Pluto and Proserpina, frolic there. But January suddenly becomes blind and despair makes him mad with jealousy. He keeps the dismayed May with him wherever he goes. Ever resourceful, however, she takes an impression of January's key in warm wax; and Damien then, with the copy he has made, lets himself into the *hortus* where he patiently waits up a tree (becoming the serpent in January's Eden). January promises to make May his sole heir and May, signalling frantically to Damien, loudly protests her honour. In an argument over the perfidy of wives, Pluto promises to restore January's sight and Proserpina promises to grant May the rhetorical powers to blind January to the truth. The pregnant May now craves to eat the pears up a certain tree and asks to stand on January's back. Clambering on top of her husband, May has sex with Damien up the tree. Pluto, at the critical moment, restores January's sight and the old man looks up only to see the unthinkable. Outraged, he accuses her but Proserpina's gift now comes to May's aid. She insists that, in order to restore his sight, she had been instructed to struggle with a man up a tree and that the blurry-eyed January uncharitably mistook an innocent struggle for something more suspect. January of course believes her and so the story ends.

The tale attempts to fix, universalize and essentialize female nature and it does this through turning the female into the artistic creation of man. The image of woman as a work of art extends beyond this one tale, and participates in a discourse that hegemonizes production – artistic, linguistic and biological – as inherently male. One of the devices by which this is achieved is the allegorization of the third section where the plot becomes universalized. According to mediaeval theory of narrative,[4] fables are tales revealing a universal truth but are themselves fantastical, for example the beast fable. The *fabula* is one of the three fundamental classifications of mediaeval plots. The other two are *historia*, a tale usually based on an actual character but frequently incorporating fabulous elements, and *argumentum*, a tale which is not true as such but which could have happened – such a tale observes a principle of verisimilitude, a mediaeval realistic mode. Into this latter category falls *The Merchant's Tale*, as fabliau. How then can it be a *fabula*?

It is the Pluto and Proserpina episode that transforms *argumentum* into *fabula*. With the advent of Pluto and Proserpina, we move into the world of the fabulous, of myth that reveals the central truths about female nature – namely, sexual depravity and deceitful, *crabbed eloquence* (IV 1203). Pluto and Proserpina are the key elements of the *fabula* for two reasons: they themselves are fantastical pagan inventions – a mythic representation of the seasons of winter and summer; and they are set into the parodied Paradise, the misogynist Garden of Eden where woman's Eve–l is confirmed as her original sin and moral inheritance. Proserpina grants deceptive eloquence to May as a gift but it has the force of an eternal sentence for "alle wommen after, for hir sake" (IV 2267).

In this *fabula* dénouement of *The Merchant's Tale*, woman – i.e. May – is seen to move away from fabliau realism[5] and turn into a figurative model, a veiled truth that must be uncovered by the reader in order to grasp the essential meaning of female nature. The tale's dénouement demands a critical response which re-enacts and enforces the phallocentric images of creativity informing the poem. In this process, both artistic creation and critical interpretation become phallocentric acts. The female becomes the work of art, the product of the Merchant's creative fantasy and the desired object of the critic, randy for meaning and certitude. The artist brings her into existence, names her and gives her meaning. Chaucer elsewhere displays an anxiety about his art being misunderstood – as in his sharp rebuke in *Chaucer's Wordes unto Adam, his Owene Scriveyn* and in his address to his own poem, *Troilus and Criseyde*:

> That thow be understonde, God I biseche!
>
> (TC V 1798)
>
> (I pray God that you may be understood correctly.)

As work of art, then, woman looks to man as her reference point and for her sense of selfhood. This is fundamental to the role portrayed for her in the Creation story – a story made much of by the Merchant:

> And herke why – I sey nat this for noght –
> That womman is for mannes helpe ywroght.
> The hye God, whan he hadde Adam maked,
> And saugh him al allone, bely-naked,
> God of his grete goodnesse seyde than,
> "Lat us now make an helpe unto this man
> Lyk to hymself"; and thanne he made hym Eve.
>
> (IV 1323–9)

(And listen why – I do not say this for nothing –
That woman is made as an helpmate for man.
The sovereign God, after he had created Adam,
And had seen him all on his own, stark naked,
In his great goodness, God then said:
"Let us now create an helper for this man
Like himself"; and then he made Eve for him.)

Adam precedes Eve and has his being independent of her.
From his prior existence she takes her definition. She has no
independent existence. Formless until defined by man, she is
made in his likeness and for his pleasure.

May's behaviour well exemplifies how she internalizes
and implicitly affirms the definition of her nature as created
by January. Despite her rebellion against her husband, she is
the product of male fashioning – a point demonstrated by the
hortus conclusus. The association between January's *hortus* and
the Garden of Eden is obvious. Less frequently observed is
the garden as a metaphor for the womb (IV 2042–52). The
parallel between May and the Virgin Mary recalls the fre-
quent iconographic setting of the Annunciation in a garden
where the lost Garden of Eden becomes reclaimed as Mary's
womb. (See, for example, Fra Angelico's *The Annunciation*,
Museo del Gesù, Cortona (*c.* 1430).) This enclosed place to
which January has sole access, where he has sex with May
and where she will enact her fall, is a garden of his own
making. Even her protest against him – her infidelity – is
enacted in his garden. She never frees herself from its deter-
mining boundaries.

It is difficult to gauge what May's motivation is at any
given point. There is, indeed, a surface logic to her actions
as suggested when she decides to take Damien as her lover
immediately after January's marital rape (IV 1955–61). However, what is notable about May is her psychological inaccessi-
bility. On the three occasions when the narrator considers
what her response was to January's lovemaking, *dubitatio* (the
rhetorical device which expresses the narrator's apparent
uncertainty) both implies her disenchantment and points to
the gap between the narrator's and May's perspectives.

But God woot what May thoughte in hir herte,
Whan she hym saugh up sittynge in his sherte,
In his nyght-cappe, and with his nekke lene;
She preyseth nat his pleyyng worth a bene.

And she obeyeth, be hire lief or looth.

How that he wroghte, I dar nat to yow telle,
Or wheither hire thoughte it paradys or helle.

(IV 1851–4; 1961; 1963–4)

(But God knows what on earth May thought to herself,
When she saw him sitting up in his shirt,
With his night-cap and scrawny neck.
His frolics didn't cut any ice with her.)

(And she obeyed, like it or not.)

(How he performed, I dare not say,
Or whether or not she thought it heaven or hell.)

Similarly there is a passivity in her initial response to Damien
after she has decided to take him as lover. Of her acceptance,
the narrator says that:

Ther lakketh noght oonly but day and place
Wher that she myghte unto his lust suffise.

(IV 1998–9)

(The only thing remaining was to fix a time and place
Where she could accommodate his desire.)

We are out of touch with May's own sexual demands. There
is no question of mutual pleasure in her relationship with
January; his interest in her body is totally masturbatory. Even
the relationship between herself and Damien is centred on his
desire. Their arboreal consummation is described quite clearly
from Damien's not May's perspective:

And sodeynly anon this Damyan
Gan pullen up the smok, and in he throng.

(IV 2352–3)

(And at once Damien
Began to hoist up her dress and in he thrust.)

May's own assertion of sexual desire is constructed within a man-made definition of her sexual identity – as the accommodator and means of male pleasure. Although her subjective viewpoint appears to be a private, freely chosen perspective it is at a deeper level a position received from without. Even the most outspoken of Chaucer's unbiddable females, the Wife of Bath, displays this complicity with received definitions of her sex:

> For al swich wit is yeven us in oure byrthe;
> Deceite, wepyng, spynnyng God hath yive
> To wommen kyndely, whil that they may lyve.
>
> (III 400–2)
> (For all such ability has been given us from birth;
> God has bestowed deceitfulness, weeping and spinning
> On all women by nature, for as long as they live.)

Not surprisingly, May's champion, Proserpina, fares no better. In her argument with Pluto about experience and authority, Proserpina challenges the belief that language can be an accurate index of subjective experience. Watching May plotting her adultery, Pluto pronounces on female perfidy (IV 2238–41). He adduces experience to prove the utterances of male authority. Proserpina rightly points out that Pluto's authority is suppressing other forms of experience – such as that of the virtuous Roman women. She redescribes authority to validate her, not Pluto's, experience. Feeling she has won the argument, she triumphantly lays claim to true self-understanding and protests against male vilification of female nature:

> I am a womman, nedes moot I speke,
> Or elles swelle til myn herte breke.
> For sithin he seyde that we been jangleresses,
> As evere hool I moote brouke my tresses,
> I shal nat spare, for no curteisye,
> To speke hym harm that wolde us vileynye.
>
> (IV 2305–10)
> (I am a woman, and therefore I must hold forth,
> Or else I'll simply swell up and explode.

> For ever since we have been accused of being liars,
> I shall never desist – no matter how rude I get –
> From badmouthing any man who would slander us.
> Cross my heart and hope to die if what I say is any lie!

On the basis of her self-knowledge as a woman, Proserpina insists that she has to speak because women are naturally talkative. And because she is naturally talkative, she is enabled to scold all men who call her a liar. But talkativeness, scolding and lying are all shades of meaning of the one word "jangleress".[6] Proserpina's argument is that because she is a jangleress, she will jangle against all who call her a jangleress. Perfectly circular logic. In her very act of objection against Pluto's accusation, she proves its authority. Proserpina too is trapped inside January's garden; its walls delimit the parameters of her own self-knowledge as well as her lexicon of protest.

This scene of a woman who opens her mouth in rebellion only to confirm everything said against her should be understood in the light of a flourishing mediaeval tradition of commonplaces about women and language. The most desirable virtue in woman's speech appears to be silence. The mediaeval preacher, John Mirk, maintains that "a mayde schuld be seen, but not herd" and offers the Virgin Mary – alleged to have spoken only four times in her life – as the ideal to be emulated.[7] Alongside this verbal rationing is the stricture against wandering the streets. *The Thewis of Gudwomen*, a late fifteenth-century poem written in Lowland Scottish dialect, recommends that woman:

> Nocht oft in stret to be wanerand;
> For wanerynge betaknis wylsumnes.[8]
> (Should not often go wandering in the streets
> For wandering is a sign of wilfulness.)

The Wife of Bath's comment that she always loved "for to walke . . . Fro hous to hous" (III 546–7) is not as innocuous, then, as it might appear.

This restriction on women's mobility parallels the attempts to control the women's linguistic mobility. These prejudices against the wanderings of female feet and tongues are in evidence in an incident at Beverly when Margery Kempe, the fifteenth-century mystic and visionary, has been locked in an upstairs room under suspicion of Lollardism:

> þan stode sche lokyng owt at a wyndown, tellyng many good talys to hem þat wolde heryn hir, in so meche þat women wept sor & seyde wyth gret heuynes of her hertys, "Alas, woman, why xalt þu be brent?"[9]
>
> (Then she stood looking out of a window, saying many edifying things to whoever would listen to her – so movingly that women wept bitterly and in the strength of their feeling said: "Alas, woman, why is it that you must be burnt?")

Margery's talking leads to the questioning (however unofficially posed) of the justice of her sentence. This response comes, significantly, from women, and the form it takes is highly affective. Denied access to the vocabulary of formal disputation, the women register their protest in tears and emotion. Noisy emotional release becomes a particularly female language – in some respects – the only noise a woman is allowed to make. In one way, it can become a new discourse, disrupting and challenging the autonomous voice of patriarchy. Thus Margery Kempe falls into "boystows wepyng" during a sermon whereon the friar ejects her saying: "I wolde þis woman wer owte of þe chirche; she noyith þe pepil" (a noisy fit of crying . . . I want this woman out of the church – she's irritating the congregation) (p. 149).

Gossiping is another potentially disruptive form of female speech. This vice is particularly prevalent in church. John Mirk relates the incident of two women gossiping in church while a devil writes down everything they say (pp. 279–80). The vision of women nattering and laughing while the preacher – male, naturally – raises his voice above their murmurs provides a good paradigm of the conflicts and repressions inherent in phallocentric discourse. The voice of male authority needs the female listener and achieves its vocal monopoly through silencing the opposition. But within the apparently single voice of patriarchy can be traced the dissonant whispers and sniggers of restive females. In the Wife of Bath, Chaucer takes the general disruptiveness of female gossip one stage further. Here, the Wife is speaking of Alisoun, her favourite gossiping partner:

> She knew myn herte, and eek my privetee,
> Bet than oure parisshe preest, so moot I thee!
> To hire biwreyed I my conseil al.
> For hadde myn housbonde pissed on a wal,
> Or doon a thyng that sholde han cost his lyf,
> To hire, and to another worthy wyf,
> And to my nece, which that I loved weel,
> I wolde han toold his conseil every deel.
> And so I dide ful often, God it woot,
> That made his face often reed and hoot
> For verray shame, and blamed hymself for he
> Had toold to me so greet a pryvetee.
>
> (III 531–42)

> (She knew my mind – and also my secrets
> Better than the parish priest, I can tell you!
> I revealed all my confessions to her.
> For even if my husband only took a piss against the wall
> Or had committed something that could cost him his life –
> I would blab all his confidences, every single last one,
> To her and to another respectable woman,
> (Not to mention my niece of whom I was rather fond.)
> And God knows I blew his cover so often
> That he was perpetually red in the face
> With mortification and he could have kicked himself
> For having shot his mouth off to me.)

In the gossip world of female discourse, suppression of unacceptable desires and behaviour has no force at all. The deepest secrets, unnameable in the language of the parish priest, are here named, shared and socially validated amongst the women. Moreover, hierarchy, a rigorously observed principle of the symbolic and social order, is levelled. The Wife recognizes no distinction between the husband's trivial secrets – such as pissing against a wall – and serious ones – such as would have cost him his life. Female discourse transgresses the sacred boundary between the public and private.

This perceived formlessness of the female finds its echo in scholastic accounts of human generation where the female is a defective male. Some defect in the foetal matter or circumstances of conception disable the sperm from reproducing itself.[10] When she rebels against male authority, as the Wife of Bath does, she therefore exhibits this innate amorphousness which undoes into shapelessness what man has created. The noisy disorder of female speech is thus only a surface aspect of a much more deep-seated, less conscious and tangible ideology which is shaping mediaeval definitions of female nature.

The very attempt to describe mediaeval female nature based on evidence such as female language is itself a male-centred project. It is, in fact, precisely what the Merchant is trying to do. Through his parody of Eden and the Fall, he reproduces woman in his own image of her. In a perfect circle of formal logic, woman becomes exactly as men have named her, through Proserpina's and May's own words.

The irony is that the self-damnation dissembles as voluntary female rebellion. By casting Proserpina's behaviour as protest against misogyny, the Merchant makes her appear to be acting freely. The manipulation of female nature is conducted at one remove. Woman falls because she chooses to do so. In orthodox terms, mediaeval woman, as a human being, must possess the faculty of free will. But over and above this generic faculty, Chaucer is quick to assert the gender-specific rights of free choice. The *Parliament of Fowls*'s formel eagle is allowed to have her "choys al fre" (free choice) (649). Criseyde shows her reluctance to take a husband, claiming that "I am myn owene womman" (*TC* II 750–6). When, then, she does take Troilus as lover, she insists that she does so of her own free choice (*TC* III 1210–11). And in *The Franklin's Tale*, the narrator insists that "wommen, of kynde, desiren libertee" (women, by nature, desire freedom) (V 768).

Chaucer's women are presented as independent and when they lose this independence – as in marriage – they appear to do so freely. Thus Dorigen, when she accepts Arveragus's insistence that she fulfil her pledge to Aurelius is doing so freely (*The Franklin's Tale*); Virginia, when she receives

death at the hands of her father is doing so freely (*The Phys-
ician's Tale*); and Griselde, when she allows Walter to kill her
children, accepts his authority freely (*The Clerk's Tale*). As
long as subordination appears voluntary and not forced then
individual female liberty and acceptance of authority are rec-
oncilable – even complementary. Free will functions as a distorting mirror, inviting the female to misrecognize herself as
the immediate shaper of her own destiny, to identify choice
with conformity.

This identification applies to her social estate but more
subtly to her innate womanliness. She was born a woman and
must therefore conform her desires, speech and behaviour to
that natural model. This conformity is achieved through
choice; of her own free will she disciplines her rebellious spirit.
This is the highest form of freedom. Such internalization of
an essential womanly nature ensures that woman will regard
her own protests against such a standard as unnatural, deviant
and untrue to her "real" self. Thus Anelida refuses to act
suitor to Arcite:

> And shal I preye, and weyve womanhede? –
> Nay! Rather deth than do so foul a dede! –
> (*Anelida and Arcite* 299–300)
> (Should I put aside my feminine role and act the suitor?
> Never! I'd rather die than sink to such depths!)

Chaucer repeatedly appeals to this idea of intrinsic
womanliness in *The Book of the Duchess* (850); in *Troilus and
Criseyde* (*TC* I 282–3, 286–7); in *The Clerk's Tale* (1083–4), to
name but a few. Nowhere is this essentialism plainer than in
The Merchant's Tale where Proserpina grants all women the gift
of verbal deception. Thus it is easy to dehistoricize female
protest by calling it archetypal misbehaviour. May commits
adultery because, like all women, she is essentially bad. This
is the Merchant's ultimate conclusive explanation. No extenu-
ating circumstances are taken into consideration; they are
irrelevant to the *sentence*.[11]

Chaucer's women lead us in a circle back to their creator
– man. The myths of Narcissus and Pygmalion are central to
the tale's dynamic of male creativity and are anticipated by

two particular references: one to a mirror; the other to wax. The Narcissus myth informs January's search for a wife and is suggested by the comparison between the old knight's mind and a mirror:

> Many fair shap and many a fair visage
> Ther passeth thurgh his herte nyght by nyght,
> As whoso tooke a mirour, polisshed bryght,
> And sette it in a commune market-place,
> Thanne sholde he se ful many a figure pace
> By his mirour; and in the same wyse
> Gan Januarie inwith his thoght devyse
> Of maydens whiche that dwelten hym bisyde.
>
> (IV 1580–7)
>
> (Many a neat little figure and pretty little face
> Passes through his musing mind during the long nights,
> Rather like someone who took a brightly-polished mirror
> And set it up in the open market-place;
> Such a person would then see many a creature passing
> Through his mirror. And in just the same way,
> January began to ponder to himself
> On various maidens who lived in the vicinity.)

These maidens are the reflections of January's mind. In them, January is really viewing himself. In an earlier passage, the narrator describes the perfect wife:

> Al that hire housbonde lust, hire liketh weel;
> She seith nat ones "nay," whan he seith "ye."
> "Do this," seith he; "Al redy, sire," seith she.
>
> (IV 1344–6)
>
> (Everything her husband likes pleases her too;
> She never crosses him with a "no" to his "yes".
> "Jump," says he. "At once, sir," says she.)

In the wife, the husband sees himself doubled. She is both his Echo and his mirror offering him his voice and image back – only this time gratifyingly empowered. Hence the references in the poem to woman being man's flesh (IV 1335; 1386).

Because of this, January claims total sexual licence in marriage:

> A man may do no synne with his wyf,
> Ne hurte hymselven with his owene knyf.
>
> (IV 1839–40)

(A man cannot fornicate with his own wife,
Nor hurt himself with his own knife.)

The phallic "knyf" is no longer an occasion for sin because January "useth" (*The Parson's Tale* 375) it with his legitimate wife and for the legitimate purpose of procreation.[12] This image of January (not) sinning with his own flesh highlights the masturbatory quality of his narcissism. The mirror image enables the man to pleasure his own flesh in woman and reproduce it in an heir.

Narcissism informs the marital enterprise. The figure of Narcissus stands behind the tale – a metaphor of male creativity. One of the most obvious accounts of Narcissus is that given in Lorris's *Roman de la Rose*[13] – a work alluded to in the description of January's garden (IV 2032). Narcissus's self-encounter also informs the artistic enterprise. January's garden contains a fountain (IV 2036) and in the French *Roman* (1423–1612), it is Narcissus's mirror-fountain into which the dreamer poet gazes and first encounters the rose – the source of both quest and poem. The artistic enterprise emerges as another form of self-seeking.

The Merchant's Tale's complementary and more dominant metaphor of phallocentric creativity is Pygmalion. Pygmalion likens the hopelessness of his love for his statue to the hopelessness of Narcissus's love for his own reflection (20846–58). Creativity in the *Roman* stems from narcissism – hence Pygmalion's motivation to create an image for his own glory (20791–5). Pygmalion works in all sorts of material – including wax (20789). His creative impulse recalls January who desires a wife he can ply like warm wax (IV 1429–1430). (May's copying of January's key in warm wax usurps this male prerogative.) The Pygmalion episode provides a direct analogue to January's marriage. Both accounts observe the same sequence of events: the elaborate wardrobes concocted for the brides (20907–83), (IV 1700); the wedding between the two couples (20984–90), (IV 1701–8); the beautiful music devised for the nuptials (20991–21028), (IV 1709–41) where, interestingly, the legendary musician Amphioun of Thebes is mentioned in both passages. And finally, both brides are conducted to the marriage bed (21029–34), (IV 1805–18); one is an unresponsive ivory statue – the other a stonily unresponsive woman:

> The bryde was broght abedde as stille as stoon.
>
> (IV 1818)
> (The bride was led to the bed – as still as stone.)

The tools, so to speak, of Pygmalion's trade are phallic. The symbolism of his hammer becomes explicit in a passage shortly before the Pygmalion episode in the *Roman* (19513ff.), where Genius speaks of the hammer, stylus and plough as images of the male generative organs – the *coillons* (testicles) and *viz* (penis) mentioned earlier by Reason (6936–7). The implements of art in the *Roman* – the hammer, the stylus – symbolize male sexual creative power. This is not to say that women cannot be artists. Thamyris and Irene in Boccaccio's *De mulieribus claris* (*Concerning Famous Women*) are both skilled artists. But Boccaccio celebrates their talent precisely because – as he claims – it is so irregular for the female to possess the artistic impulse. Pygmalion's act of artistic creation becomes the act of sex. Just as he gives definition to the shapeless passive ivory, so the poet, with his phallic stylus, inscribes his meaning upon the blank page of womanhood, engendering words. In *The Merchant's Tale*, we can trace the myth of phallocentric creativity back through January, through Narcissus, through Pygmalion, back to the Garden of Eden. The Pygmalion impulse to create woman in his likeness exactly parallels the divine impulse to create: "*In gloriam meam creavi eum, formavi eum, et feci eum*" ("I have created him for my glory, I have fashioned him and I have made him") (Isaiah 43.7).

If the mediaeval act of artistic creation is constructed as the act of sex, then conversely the act of sex implies phallocentric creativity. *The Merchant's Tale* refers to the young wife "on which he myghte engendren hym an heir" (IV 1272). Compare the use of the phrase "begat upon", in, for example, "Melibeus . . . begat upon his wyf" his daughter Sophie (VII 967–8) and in the *Legend of Good Wommen*, where the narrator says of Jason and Hypsipyle that "upon hire begat he children two" (1562). The male is the active creator, the woman the passive receptacle. Women's capacity to conceive is obliterated by a theory of physiology which defines the semen as the active, life-giving seed and the female egg, or sometimes menstrual matter, as the passive material on which that seed works.[14]

The woman of the Fall turns out to be a monster who, in this tale, commits a multiple symbolic castration of her own "creator". The first "castration" takes the form of the blindness administered by the goddess Fortune. Traditionally portrayed as female, and typically female in her fickleness, Fortune sums up the darker aspects of female sexuality:

> O sodeyn hap! O thou Fortune unstable!
> Lyk to the scorpion so deceyvable,
> That flaterest with thyn heed whan thou wolt stynge;
> Thy tayl is deeth, thurgh thyn envenymynge.
> O brotil joye! O sweete venym queynte!
> O monstre, that so subtilly kanst peynte
> Thy yiftes under hewe of stidefastnesse,
> That thou deceyvest bothe moore and lesse!
>
> (IV 2057–64)
>
> (What an unforeseen calamity! Oh, inconstant Fortune!
> You're like the treacherous scorpion,
> That flatters with its head just as it's about to sting.
> Death is in its tail with its fatal poison.
> What fickle pleasure! What sweet deceptive venom!
> What a monster, who can so cunningly disguise
> Your favours with a veneer of constancy,
> So that you deceive everyone.)

"Queynte", though here primarily meaning "deceptive", is suggestive of the Middle English word "cunte".[15] The image of Fortune anticipates precisely May's flattering of January with her head whilst preparing her tail to deliver the sting of adultery.

January's second "castration" is that of being cuckolded. In his marital Paradise, his eyes are literally opened to May's sin. Innocence yields to experience, to the knowledge that his inner sanctum, May's womb, has been invaded by another man's seed. He has been robbed of his property rights in May and of his sexual treasure – a surrogate castration. The encounter shows how the attempt of the "creator" to possess exclusively and absolutely what he has created leads him inadvertently to confront that unbridgeable gap between himself and his reflection. Narcissus's mirror of art cracks from side to side.

In January's final "castration", May blinds his mental sight, depriving him of reason and authority – the emblems of his manhood and husbandly estate. Just as Adam listened to his wife so January does to May. The hierarchical inversion is foreshadowed when May stands on top of January to climb the pear tree; wife tops husband; woman tops man; passion tops reason. This picture of Chaucer's women seems a sombre one, where female nature, even in its acts of rebellion, is determined by its male creator. *The Merchant's Tale* implicitly claims the creative act as essentially male. But May, like the Wife of Bath, is also an artist, a weaver of words – only she inverts the process, turning truth into fiction and reality into appearance. In being created, she undoes the male creative process; she confounds the phallocentric quest for certitude with deceptions, and blurs distinctions between truth and falsehood, reality and appearance. If it is true that May damns herself with her own lying language it is also true that she gets the last word – not, no doubt, what the Merchant, January, Narcissus, Pygmalion, Pluto, God – or even, perhaps, Chaucer – ever intended.

How William Carlos Williams Gave Birth

Alison Smith

Some Critical Responses

There are many received critical commonplaces about the American poet William Carlos Williams. He is master of the glimpse, the poet who turns the caught moment of seeing an old woman eating plums out of a bag, or a girl taking off her shoe in the street, or a piece of brown paper blowing over and over, into an epiphanic poetic moment. He is master of the objective gaze, at things like a wheelbarrow or certain flowers, or a cat climbing with careful precision into a flowerpot. He is the poet who rejects symbolism, simile, metaphor. He is so interested in objectivity in the gaze that at one point in his life he helped form a group calling itself Objectivist, and the members of this group took the power of objectivity further and set out to define the poem too as a separate object. He is the poet for whom a main poetic theme was spring and the promise and possibilities of endless new beginnings.[1] And he is known as the poet of the 1920s locality debate, who publicly fought for a localized American art rather than one too influenced by European art.

But Williams, of course, is most notoriously known for his much repeated phrase, "no ideas but in things". This personalized aesthetic statement turns up in his poetry and prose from 1927 onwards[2] and is accepted critically as his adopted philosophical talisman, rather like "rose is a rose . . . " is accepted as Stein's. But where Stein's phrase points out in a way exactly how a word may be defamiliarized in a unit of language, split away from what it refers to in its repeated circling, "no ideas but in things" is a phrase that won't let referent be split from reference, or abstract from physical, or word from thing. "No ideas but in things" advocates a rejection of the solely metaphysical, rejects idea that's not somehow attached to thing.

And for a long time Williams's proclaimed rejection of idea unless attached to thing has allowed critics to reject him as anti-intellectual, really rather naïve and world-enthusiastic, writing a poetry of exclamation marks and exuberant outbursts; a poetry, what's more, where *too* much depends upon the red wheelbarrow. Take the poet James Fenton's fairly recent attack on Williams for the "banality" of his work:

> the obvious fault, as with so much imagist and projectivist verse, is the banality of the aesthetic stance. Pay attention to things! says the poet, they are so amazingly *thingy*. The phenomenal world . . . it's *phenomenal*![3]

In this there's another oft-found critical reaction to Williams: critical dismissal of his exclamatory amazement at the things and the world of external reality. Even J. Hillis Miller, who so keenly championed Williams's experiments with the relationship between words and things in his 1966 text, *Poets of Reality*, has stated more recently that there are peculiar critical problems in facing a poetry that so denies abstraction:

> my fascination with and admiration for William Carlos Williams is . . . that Williams is so resistant to intellectualizing. He is a very great poet, but difficult for somebody trained in abstractions. I can deal with ideas, and the thing itself, and so on – no problem – but what do you say about "The Red Wheelbarrow" or about a poem that just describes a sycamore tree?[4]

So. Fenton finds it banal to appreciate your surroundings with the exclamation marks and renewing amazement of a poet like Williams and feels that, in any case, there's nothing *said* by a poetry that engages in this way with the world of things. Miller feels there's nothing to *say* about such a poetry, and goes on to comment on how it's much easier to write on a poet like Wallace Stevens, someone who's "especially open to academic criticism". One more stock response then, and it's the warm but excuse-making response of those who see Williams as the naïve lover-of-life, the anti-intellectual prophet, the sentimentalized champion of the overlooked. Here's a typical comment, one that smacks somewhat of the patronizing tone of obituary columns, from the critic Bram Dijkstra:

> [Williams] may not always have understood what he saw, but in his bright joy for the shape of things, and in his fiery determination to lift the small beauties of our everyday environment to the center of our vision, he has indeed given the world a most valuable legacy.[5]

It seems to me that none of these responses examines what's clearly the most pressing question in Williams's work. Why is this poet so clearly determined, so desperate (and I'd emphasize the desperation) to make the link so strong between poem and thing, and poem and world, so keen to outline connections in his work between abstract idea and physical thing?

Some Ideas About the Connection Between Ideas and Things

Williams wrote hundreds of poems. And throughout his life Williams suggested repeatedly that each poem as an artefact has an existence of its own and is as much a separate object or physical artefact as a bridge, an apple, a painting (and this is an idea not a million miles away from Eliot's assertion in *The Sacred Wood* that art has its own separate living, breathing existence). In 1919 he talks of poetry as "made by the hands of the poet out of nothing", seeing the poet as some godlike creator. In 1923 the notion of a poem as a separate entity, a made thing, is central to the prose of his collection, *Spring and All*. Here, art, he says, is "not a matter of 'representation' . . .

but of separate existence", here "works of art . . . must be real, not 'realism' but reality itself". In *Spring and All* he also makes clear a difference he believes there to be between poetry and prose, a difference made precisely by poetry's having some separate existence in "reality". Poetry was "to do with the dynamization of emotion into a separate form", a "new form dealt with as a reality in itself", while prose remained a mere "statement of facts". By the end of the twenties "once the writing is on the paper it becomes an object". And by 1957, a few years before his death, Williams typically wrote, "a poem is a complete little universe. It exists separately".[6]

The terms that Williams consistently uses are fascinating – the poet, in and on his own terms, has been the *maker of something separate* for practically the whole of his poetic career. To turn now to how these terms are put to use in the poetic act, I'd like to look closely at a typical poem from Williams's 1921 collection, *Sour Grapes*. "The Cold Night" appears in the collection at the end of a run of cold winter poems. If there is a notable theme in Williams's work it's the rejuvenatory effect of rebirth that the three different creative powers of sex, spring and poetry can have, and in "The Cold Night" Williams offers some "answers" to the barren season of winter.

> It is cold. The white moon
> is up among her scattered stars –
> like the bare thighs of
> the Police Sergeant's wife – among
> her five children . . .
> No answer. Pale shadows lie upon
> the frosted grass. One answer:
> It is midnight, it is still
> and it is cold . . . !
> White thighs of the sky! a
> new answer out of the depths of
> my male belly: In April . . .
> In April I shall see again – In April!
> the round and perfect thighs
> of the Police Sergeant's wife
> perfect still after many babies.
> Oya![7]

Remember here that one of the most popular critical common-places about Williams is his rejection of metaphor for the direct treatment of the thing in the poem. Hillis Miller, Dijkstra and Charles Doyle, among others, have all written at length on his rejection of symbol, simile, and particularly metaphor. A typical comment:

> simile, analogy and metaphor he rejected as inappropriate to his sense of "the poem", preferring to assert the necessity of keeping one's eye on the object.[8]

A close look at this poem will reveal that although Williams was keen to reject simile, he hardly rejected metaphor. On the contrary, metaphor is everywhere in his work, and here at the centre of "The Cold Night", the poem in search of answers, metaphor is the rejuvenating power. Here it is not enough to say "the white moon/is up among her scattered stars – /*like* the bare thighs of/the Police Sergeant's wife", this is "no answer" to winter, and all that can follow it is the image of pale shadows and frosted glass. Simile is rejected as not powerful enough. "One answer", however, lies in seeing what is directly there, what is, as in some way wondrous, something to exclaim about: "One answer:/It is midnight, it is still/and it is cold . . . !". But there is an even better answer to come on the cold night, a better version than the plain "it is", and one that seems prompted by it. The original simile is turned into the exulting, humorous exclamation of metaphor in "White thighs of the sky!", the Lorca-like fusion of poetic and physical properties welded into metaphor.

Now this metaphor is termed "a/new answer out of the depths of/my male belly". This is a new kind of fertility. This is a man's pregnancy in a poem that's ostensibly about a woman's pregnancy, about birth. And, following the logic of the poem, this male pregnancy is what frees the "answer", allows spring to break in at the end of the poem with the intimations of April and the image of renewed seeing ("in April I shall see again – in April") of things on the cold night. The final exclamation is the eureka, the breakthrough, of the poem, the return of spring.

"The Cold Night", then, can be seen to be about the

male birth of the poem, a new answer out of the depths of the male belly. The poem about childbirth becomes concerned with artistic conception at the same time, concerned with the way things are put, the way they're arranged or said, examining the movement from simile through direct presentation of the thing to a *fusion* that's inherent in metaphor. The poem's displayed discovery and use of metaphor brings about visions or promises of physical birth and seasonal rebirth, where simply saying an objective "it is" wasn't enough. There is something more than objectivity happening here, and in a way it's related to gender limits and possibilities.

Sex and Metaphor: The Urgency of Contact

Williams was of course Dr Williams, full time M.D. and spare moment poet, who reportedly flipped up his typewriter in the surgery and dashed off poetry between patients. Much of his medical life was spent in the role of obstetrician, and he helped give birth to thousands of babies in his lifetime. Birth is a precious word in his lexicon, particularly the birth of a clean renewed language, washed of all old nuances. It's a theme of a great number of his poems, most famously "By the road to the contagious hospital", the first poem of *Spring and All*. And of course, Williams was keen to help bring to birth a localized art for America.[9]

Ezra Pound was one of the American writers Williams accused of defecting to Europe, running away from the American problem of creating an art that would validate the American locality. Pound was one of the early influential advisers to Williams on the subject of his poetic development, suggesting that he reject his early Keatsian inversions, his Palgraveian rhyming forms, and keep his poetic syntax close to that of natural speech. He advised him too to subscribe to the adventurous European and American little magazines, which Williams did, and published Williams's poetry in the magazines where he had influence. They remained argumentative friends until Williams's death, Williams always castigating the defector.

In his *Autobiography* Williams wrote of the particular influence of Pound the poet that he was keen *not* to accept:

what I could never tolerate in Pound or seek for myself
was the "side" that went with all his posturings as the
poet. To me that was the emptiest sort of old hat. . . . My
upbringing assumed rather the humility and caution of
the scientist. One was or one was not *there*.[10]

As poetic postures go, basic existence is a fundamental point
in that of Williams, the fundamentality of either being or not
being *there*. This is why Williams is so concerned to make his
immediate surroundings or locality aesthetically valid and
accepted; this is why he is so concerned with the locality called
the backyard, or Paterson New Jersey, or America; he is
centrally concerned with the locality of being there.

Pound wrote often with a sharp insight about Williams's
work, but never sharper than when he wrote a letter in 1917
needling Williams regarding his proclaimed demands about
duty to an aesthetic of locality. In this letter, Pound intelli-
gently noticed a *lack of confidence in identity* at the basis of
Williams's attachment to the creation of such an aesthetic.
"If you had any confidence in America you wouldn't be so
touchy about it".[11]

"The love of the actual underlies all American enjoy-
ment", wrote Williams, outlining what to him is a markedly
American response, an American love.[12] It's clear that Williams's poetry is troubled by a peculiar urgency. And in his
poetry the "love of the actual", said by him to be so based in
place, is peculiarly gender based in both poetic theme and
practice. Thom Gunn, writing recently on the publication of
the first volume of the newly edited *Collected Poems* of William
Carlos Williams, deftly described Williams's poetic impetus
and technique: "it is as if he woos the physical world".[13]
Certainly the 1920 poem, "Portrait of a Lady", clearly reveals
the presence of the poet making metaphor as a way of making
love.

> Your thighs are appletrees
> whose blossoms touch the sky.
> Which sky? The sky
> where Watteau hung a lady's
> slipper. Your knees

are a southern breeze – or
a gust of snow. Agh! what
sort of man was Fragonard?
– as if that answered
anything. Ah, yes – below
the knees, since the tune
drops that way, it is
one of those white summer days,
the tall grass of your ankles
flickers upon the shore –
Which shore? –
the sand clings to my lips –
Which shore?
Agh, petals maybe. How
should I know?
Which shore? Which shore?
I said petals from an appletree.[14]

"Portrait of a Lady" is a self-defined work of art, with its
ringing references to Henry James and T.S. Eliot. Here the
lady's aesthetic presence, or portrait, is created wholly out of
the male response. At the same time the poem acts out a
merging of sensual, natural and aesthetic reference so that
self-assertion is negated and personal detail left behind,
"what/sort of man was Fragonard?/– as if that answered/
anything". The man who gives the woman her body made of
metaphors writes himself into self-forgetfulness, in the giving
over or entering in of self to the head-spinning sexual experience of both lady and artistic creation – writes himself *away*
from the problem of identity. In 1921, a year after writing this
poem, Williams sent a letter to a young poet advising him
how to go about writing more successful poetry:

> if only you would forget yourself in a wild burst of compo-
> sition, building up a structure without any thought but
> for the development of what you see and feel when a girl
> of the type you praise passes you – it would be worth
> something. Build it up like a pleasure house.[15]

Composition here becomes a hedonism, a pleasurable structure, something which can itself be sexually termed, a "wild burst" of desirous or aroused self-negation. Williams continues in the same letter: "my liking is for an unimpeded thrust right through a poem from the beginning to the end, without regard to formal arrangements". His enthusiasm for this "thrust" is a part of the anarchic disregard of formal design found throughout his work. As he commented, late in life, "the rhythmic pace was . . . an excited pace because I was excited when I wrote".[16] There's an attraction in the giving over and the entering in of the self to the poetic experience.

In 1929 the *Little Review* held a special edition where they published the answers they had received from several writers and artists responding to a circulated questionnaire. Question number ten, the final question, asked "Why do you go on living?". Williams's answer to this question was "because I have an enjoyable body for my pleasure", the ultimate pagan answer to existence.[17] In one issue of *Contact*, the little magazine he founded and coedited, Williams wrote a thinly veiled anonymous piece about a young stud called Evan Dionysius Evans (EDE if not WCW) who is visited at night in his bed by a beautiful "gleaming and naked" young woman who turns out to be an embodiment of America, in comparison to the embodiment of Europe, an old syphilitic bitch gone in the teeth who also solicits his attention and who is turned down. "At least, ventured Evan D. Evans to himself, the American hussey [*sic*] has a great future before her".[18] American identity is translated into this sexually promising vision, the woman waiting to be inseminated, and Williams continues to associate his America, his "*nuevo mundo*", the land waiting to be aesthetically discovered and validated, with the image of the young waiting virgin, in books like *In the American Grain* (1925) and *The Great American Novel* (1923).

Contact, the early twenties magazine edited by Williams and Robert McAlmon, was devoted to the cultivation of locality in art, and was above all concerned with the notion of contact – connection, interrelation, in actual contact, actual touch. To quote its editorial manifesto: "in explaining his position in America" the artist should use "the sensual accidents of his immediate contacts", these "sensual accidents" would make a "locus" and this locus "will put his work on a comparable basis with the best work created abroad". In *Contact* this definition of "locus" is never far from sexual reference; achieving locus is described as the "separate implantation of the sperm".[19] This sexual definition of the aesthetic aim is deep in Williams's work of the time; as he wrote in *The Great American Novel* (1923), "to progress from word to word is to suck a nipple".[20] Now this metaphoric link between art and physical pleasure, and between sex and the fundamental act of reading or writing from word to word, suggestive here of reproduction, maternal nurturing and pleasurable sensation, is at the base of the eagerness and sensual immediacy of his work, and perhaps at the base of the urgency which is also associated with the exclamatory voice of his early poetry. A poem like "April", written in 1921, will stand as a typical example of this, with its typical spring theme and its typical dionysian quick-breathing "pounding", its "too many opening hearts of lilac leaves,/too many, too many swollen/limp poplar tassels on the/bare branches!". "I had no rest against that/springtime!", the poet exclaims at the end of the poem. "I awoke smiling but tired".[21]

There is an urgency in the poem "April", and it can be closely aligned with the general sense of urgency in the demanding voice of Williams's early work, a voice that often exclaims "I must tell you", "we must listen", "so much depends upon". In Williams's work the building of the pleasure house structure of the poem is partly the drive behind such urgency. But, as Williams said, "no one writes if he doesn't have to".[22] In the stating of the necessity for contact, an urgency is discerned that can be traced, as I will show, to a search for confidence or security in gendered identity.

What Good Poetry is Made of

It is not widely known or noted that in 1917 Williams wrote two lengthy philosophical letters to the London-based periodical *The Egoist*, addressing himself to a debate stirred up by Dora Marsden's opaque articles on "lingual psychology", articles examining the possibility of a separate female language, philosophy and psychology. I would like to draw attention to these letters, published in April and August of 1917, particularly to the latter of these.[23] They offer sharp insight into the poet of reality's notions of the relation of gender to the "reality" to which he is determined to attach his ideas.

In these letters Williams, who has clearly been annoyed at Dora Marsden's summary dismissal of interest in a *male* lingual psychology, states that, like Marsden, he believes there to be two definedly separate psychologies, a male and a female. (Both Williams and Marsden had been particularly influenced by Otto Weininger's popular 1906 book, *Sex and Character*, where Weininger presents such a gendering of separate psychologies.) Williams, interchanging "psychology" and "philosophy" as he pleases, stating that it's the distinction between male and female that he is interested in, takes issue with Marsden, he says, because of the sterility of her posited argument. You can't have female without male, one psychology, or philosophy is sterilely incomplete without the other, according to Williams. He underlines the necessary fusion, the coming together, of the separate male and female processes, a fusion which, he insists, produces *all* forms of creativity including the cerebral:

> life, in the realm of thought as in all other realms of activity, is the first essential, and to maintain life two things are necessary – which, I repeat, Miss Marsden has taken into consideration but without realizing their full significance: a male and a female element: an engendering force and a definite point of action.

Here the male is the "force", and the female the "definite point" to be acted upon. And it's here that Williams, the poet so well known as renowned rejector of the metaphysical, champion and poet of the real, reveals an extraordinary insecurity. "Reality", he says, actually "differs for the two sexes". He goes on to suggest that there is "universal lack of attachment between the male and an objective world – to the earth under his feet", and this is because "the male, aside from his extremely simple sex function, is wholly unnecessary to objective life".

Women, however, are different. "Female psychology . . .

is characterized by a trend not away from but toward the earth, toward concreteness", writes the poet so fascinated by concreteness that he wants to create his own solid objects of poems. Women, according to Williams, are particularly attached to this concrete reality by what he calls "definite physical results". Woman's "pursuit of the male" produces "definite physical results that connect her indisputably and firmly with the earth at her feet by an unalterable chain, every link of which is concrete". Women can have these "definite physical results" or, in other words, babies. Williams then outlines man's place in this scheme of things: "man's only positive connexion with the earth is in the fleeting sex function. When not in pursuit of the female man has absolutely no necessity to exist".

Having "absolutely no necessity to exist", being "wholly unnecessary to objective life" – these must surely be the most devastating and central dilemmae for the poet who later sums up his poetic position as "one was or one was not *there*". Here, man must be "in pursuit of the female" to have any meaningful existence at all.

Thirty years later Williams was still seeing the sexes as ultimately separate and destined to "an impossibility of meeting". In 1948 Williams wrote his essay "Woman as Operator" for a collection of essays called *Women: a Collaboration of Artists and Writers*, where writers from Williams to Sartre responded to the visual images of women in a contemporary art exhibition.[24] Williams's essay is complex in tone, a mixture of admiration for and hostility towards not women, but Woman. For by the time of writing this, he has come to a further conclusion as regards gender. "Woman doesn't have to be so particularized" as men do:

> when she stands on her feet, any woman, it is woman standing on her feet whereas if it is a man you immediately say, What man? . . . every portrait of some woman comes out as woman, every portrait of man comes out as some man – or nothing.

Man's identity is still tenuous to him, an affair of being particularized, or "nothing". And to avoid being nothing, man must assert his individual identity, be "some man", and this assertion is a particularly male process. "Man has to be identified (to save himself)", Williams continues, "so he goes on painting all his life, developing his art". (Art, for Williams here, is a specifically male domain.) In fact he reveals in "Woman as Operator", that woman is "unassailable", out of men's control:

> What is he to do? Impregnate her? Kill her? Avoid her? You see, it all amounts to the same thing: do what he will she remains in spite of his greatest doing or not doing the same thing, woman, woman in the abstract, something without a face, something beyond his power.

(Later he comments on the only way to destroy woman: "woman is never destroyed by man, but always by the child".)

The notion of the creative artist's territory as a specifically male territory is strongly foreshadowed in Williams's idiosyncratic version of American history, *In The American Grain*. Despite his admiration of the work of Marianne More and Mina Loy, it seems clear here that women, to Williams, somehow can't really inherit the ability to be poets; this is certainly one of the differences he makes between the genders in the chapter called "Jacataqua".

> Poets? Where? They are the test. But a true woman in flower, never. Emily Dickinson, starving of passion in her father's garden, is the very nearest we have ever been – starving .... Never a woman: never a poet .... Oh, men have had women, millions of them, of course: good firm Janes. But one that spouted any comprehensive joy? Never.[25]

Women can't "spout comprehensive joy", women can't be poets, not really virile poets. Emily Dickinson was that unusual thing, a woman poet, and in the face of this Williams emphasizes an image of Dickinson as a cooped up frustrated old maid, and her father's daughter rather than someone in her own right.

Two years earlier, in *The Great American Novel*, Williams

had rewritten a well known children's rhyme to fit his definition of what makes good poetry:

> And what is good poetry made of
> And what is good poetry made of
> Of rats and snails and puppy dog's tails
> And that is what good poetry is made of
>
> And what is bad poetry made of
> And what is bad poetry made of
> Of sugar and spice and everything nice
> That is what bad poetry is made of.[26]

In this there is a clear though subdued gender dismissal, even hostility. It looks to be declaring that the best poetry should be removed from niceness, sweetness and gentility and can be found in the raw, the vulgar, the fascination for the "anti-poetic", as Wallace Stevens called it,[27] that runs in Williams's work. But underneath this, could this rhyme suggest that boys are best, boys can and girls can't write good poetry by nature?

It seems that this needed creative and difficult fusion of male and female elements is a very early concern of the poet. A 1914 poem called "Transitional" considers this fusion as central to the writing impetus, and even suggests a third state of being, a third, privileged being, neither male nor female:

> First he said:
> It is the woman in us
> That makes us write –
> Let us acknowledge it –
> Men would be silent.
> We are not men
> Therefore we can speak
> And be conscious
> (of the two sides)
> Unbent by the sensual
> As befits accuracy.
>
> I then said:
> Dare you make this
> Your propaganda?

And he answered:
Am I not I – here?[28]

Here the poem presents a specifically male discussion where
men take on the power that "belongs" to women and by doing
so move into a "transitional" gender state. Here the poet
questions the speaker, who is a writer, or an honorary comprehensive fusion of male and female elements. The poem ends
on the assertion of the fusion being the assertion of the individual self, the assertion of the defined existence of man on
earth, in place, in the rhetorical question, "am I not I –
here?".

The writer here, then, is *more* than just a man; he is an
embodiment of the necessary fusion of those two elements of
male and female, which, when put together, allow for
creativity. The short poem "Marriage", written in 1916, states
the difference between the sexes:

So different, this man
And this woman:
A stream flowing
In a field.[29]

If man is the "stream", the fluid and insubstantial energy
flowing through the unmoving "field", then at least poetry
can be a male birth, the production of a poem as a concrete
object. And more – the transformationary act of metaphor
can bring them naturally together.

The same transformational power of metaphor works in
the poem "Youth and Beauty", from the collection *Sour Grapes*.
Like "The Cold Night", this poem also appropriates birth,
creating offspring for the poet through personification, or
metaphor, applied to common thing:

I bought a dishmop –
having no daughter –
for they had twisted
fine ribbons of shining copper
about white twine
and made a tousled head

> of it, fastened it
> upon a turned ash stick
> slender at the neck
> straight, tall –
> when tied upright
> on the brass wallbracket
> to be a light for me
> and naked
> as a girl should seem
> to her father.[30]

With applied metaphor, the poet can make the daughter he doesn't have; with chosen words the dishmop becomes a naked daughter for the poet, created out of the meeting of poem and thing.

And this, in short, is how William Carlos Williams gives birth.

The Poetic Pursuit

Poetry for Williams certainly involves something of the nature of "pursuit of the female" which he sees as so necessary to male existence in the *Egoist* letters. Late in life he recalled, "somehow poetry and the female sex were allied in my mind . . . I knew nothing at all about the sexual approach but I had to do something about it. I did it in the only terms I knew, through poetry".[31] Remember "Portrait of a Lady" here, where to kiss the lady – with appletrees for thighs, southern breeze for knees, tall grass for ankles, in the poet's polite but sensual descent of her legs, coming away at the end with sand on his lips – to kiss, by metaphor, the woman, is to kiss the earth.

In the face of such a sense of man's tenuous involvement in natural creativity, creativity is the central theme and driving force of Williams's poetry. As he writes about the paradox of man's idiosyncratic individuality alongside his "nothingness", it is not surprising that there is an urgency in much of his work to make contact between words and things. It is not surprising either that he seeks out a poetic of "reality" in its most basic or backyard forms, its most local manifestations, not surprising that he rejects the disconnected metaphysical. With his developing notion of the poem as a separate thing, his claiming of separate actual existence for poems as artefacts, he is determinedly creating his own additions to reality.

Look for instance at the poem "Young Sycamore". William Carlos Williams is the poet who, rather than just describing the tree, as J. Hillis Miller rather lamely puts it, actually gives a body to a tree in his poem, personifies it, by metaphor gives it a body. He is the poet through whose eyes the sight of the familiar or unnoticed becomes renewed, reborn, given a spatial existence. This is after all a generous art *and* a colonizing art, one that works as a two-way assertion. It asserts and celebrates the concrete world (that thing so alien to men) and at the same time woos it, enters it, embodies it in the imaginative act. This embodying, in turn, asserts the existence of the perceiver, the new creator, new procreator, the poet, the man. For poetry, of course, is a pursuit of men. Women, according to Williams, that most objective of poets, have no need of it.

Connections and Alliances

Metaphor and Place in *To the Lighthouse*: Some Hebridean Connections

Jane Goldman

"Lies will flow from my lips"
Virginia Woolf, *A Room of One's Own*[1]

This essay explores two aspects of Woolf's novel, *To the Lighthouse*, hitherto neglected by Woolf criticism. One is metaphor: Woolf's engagement with the patriarchal enslavement of woman as metaphor. The other is place: the novel's Hebridean setting, and the literary and aesthetic implications of Woolf's choice of the Island of Skye as its context. These two aspects are interrelated, and I want to suggest how readings based on metaphor and place affect interpretations of Mrs Ramsay and Mrs McNab by encouraging readers to take seriously the Scottish setting of *To the Lighthouse*.[2] Traditional Woolf criticism has failed to acknowledge the significance of this novel's setting, and has made some serious errors when referring to it. This essay establishes that early and influential responses by critics such as David Daiches are mistaken in dismissing as inaccurate Woolf's Hebridean allusions.

Metaphor

All art that is not against its time is for it. Such art can make the time pass, but it cannot conquer it. The true enemy of time is language. Language lives in harmonious union with the spirit in revolt against its own time. Out of this conspiracy art is conceived. In contrast, conform-

ity, in complicity with its time, robs language of its own vocabulary. Art can come only from denial. Only from anguished protest. Never from calm compliance. Art placed in the service of consoling man becomes a curse unto his very deathbed. True art reaches its fulfillment only through the hopeless.
Karl Kraus, 1912[3]

Speaking on the recent Channel 4 programme, *Without Walls*, Tom Paulin made a vitriolic attack on Woolf and her work, condemning her as a conformist and her work as complicit with an old order *status quo*. He described her "outlook on life" as "narrow, élitist, even reactionary", while one of his guests on the programme, Angela Carter, regarded Woolf's novel, *Orlando*, as "the apotheosis of brown-nosing . . . to a member of the upper classes".[4]

I begin with this emphasis on critical prejudice to suggest that it might explain the neglect of the Hebridean setting in *To the Lighthouse*. The assumption that Woolf does not look further than her own supposedly restricted and élitist environment prevents some critics from looking further afield. Before we set off on the somewhat stormy journey to Woolf's Hebrides, however, I must establish the basis of my metaphorical interpretation of this novel. *To the Lighthouse*, I suggest, is structured around the disappearance of a tree from Lily Briscoe's painting. Lily in fact produces two paintings – one started in the first pre-war part of the novel and never resolved, the other started and completed (to its author's satisfaction) in the final third part. The tree which Lily, in some considerable artistic anguish, decides to move to the centre of her first picture as its final aesthetic resolution, is entirely absent from the second painting. It has been replaced. The final lines of *To the Lighthouse* describe not a tree but a line at its centre:

> With a sudden intensity, as if she saw it clear for a second, she drew a line there, in the centre. It was done; it was finished. Yes, she thought, laying down her brush in extreme fatigue, I have had my vision. (p. 320)

I do not see this much-cited moment of modernist epiphany

as an entirely abstract, aesthetic, religious, mystical, or purely emotional one, but as first and foremost a political one. The disappearance of the tree marks an important moment in Woolf's extensive and compelling engagement with the (sexual) politics and aesthetics of metaphor. Bakhtin's description of metaphor selection as born out of social interaction is a helpful starting-point for examining Woolf's engagement with the allegorical:

> The simple selection of an epithet or metaphor is already an active evaluating act, oriented in two directions – towards the listener and towards the hero [the topic of the utterance]. *The listener and the hero are the constant participants in the event of creation*, which never for an instant ceases to be an event of living interaction between them.[5] (Bakhtin's italics)

This approach fits well with a reading of Lily's painting as a product of social rather than entirely individual creation, since the novel is clearly examining the social and political context in which her art is produced. Benjamin's definition of allegories as being "in the realm of thoughts what ruins are in the realm of things" is useful for looking at Woolf's work. His notion, connected to this, of the artist as one "who could manipulate models with sovereign skill",[6] is applicable to Lily Briscoe's (and indeed Woolf's) handling and modification of allegorical figures. Derrida's very different work on "light" and "house" as the supreme metaphors, the metaphors of metaphor, is also helpful to this approach (see "White Mythology"),[7] given that Woolf's novel addresses both these terms. But Derrida does not address that other metaphor of metaphor(s) which is so central to Woolf's novel – woman.

Marina Warner's book, *Monuments and Maidens: the Allegory of the Female Form*, provides a helpful analysis of Western cultural obsessions with woman as metaphorical space. Warner remarks on the central paradox of this tradition:

> Often the recognition of a difference between the symbolic order, inhabited by ideal, allegorical figures, and the actual order, of judges, statesmen, soldiers, philosophers,

inventors, depends on the unlikelihood of women practising the concepts they represent.[8]

It is against the very feminization of the outward and visible form of metaphor that Woolf's writing is pitched; and her search for "a room of one's own" is clearly a search for a metaphoricity which does not always (and already) exclude "her". A woman's metaphorical place is neither inside nor outside, but actually constitutes metaphor's mediating and containing boundary. In traditional terms woman is seen as always the vehicle and never the tenor. Woman is the space/ room – that which expresses and contains but cannot be expressed; that which embodies but never acts – the mediator between masculine subject and material object.

In *A Room of One's Own*,[9] Woolf simultaneously foregrounds and attempts to shake off the notion of the female form as naturally given metaphorical vehicle or allegory. Woolf herself cannot deliver her lecture in the conventional first person – " 'I' is only a convenient term for somebody who has no real being" (p. 7) – so she playfully resorts to the appropriation of a number of female personae: "Here then was I (call me Mary Beton, Mary Seton, Mary Carmichael or by any name you please – it is not a matter of any importance)" (p. 8). Woolf is highlighting (and satirizing) the arbitrary manner in which the female form, effaced and displaced, is appropriated as cover for the (masculine) subject – the trinity of Marys giving all the ambiguity of a biblical emphasis to this role of compliant hostess. In the course of the book, however, these women emerge as far from interchangeable textual and cultural gaps, for Woolf surreptitiously weaves biographical snippets about them into her text (see pp. 28, 56, 120ff.). In so doing, she is enacting the advice given by "Mary Beton" to "Mary Carmichael": "Above all, you must illumine your own soul with its profundities and its shallows . . . and say what is your relation to the ever-changing and turning world of gloves and shoes and stuffs" (p. 142). This passage links the female form as allegory with the commodification of women. The woman writer is being encouraged to fill in, occupy her own space/gap – to show "the thing in itself". The near impossibility (not to mention indecent narcissism) of this strange act of contortion is not lost on Woolf; but she presents it as an historically necessary moment in the evolution of "Shakespeare's sister". Mary Carmichael "will be a poet", says Mary Beton, "in another hundred years' time" (p. 142).

A Room of One's Own was first published in 1929, two years after *To the Lighthouse*, enabling us to think of Mary Carmichael as a witty retrospective gloss on Mr Carmichael, the poet who stalks the novel as a sort of inverted muse figure to Lily Briscoe. But it was only after I had begun to think "Scottish" about *To the Lighthouse*, that the origin of Woolf's three Marys struck me as significant. It is, of course, a very famous Scottish ballad: "The Queen's Marie" or "Mary Hamilton". "The Queen's Marie", published for the first time by Walter Scott in his *Minstrelsy of the Scottish Border*, was probably the one known to Woolf. The ballad tells the story of one of the four "Maries" in attendance on the Queen: Mary Hamilton is discovered to have murdered her own baby, born from an illicit affair at court, and is sentenced to death. From the gallows (in Edinburgh) she exclaims:

> "Yestreen the queen had four Maries,
>   The night she'll hae but three;
> There was Marie Seaton, and Marie Beaton,
>   And Mary Carmichael, and me."[10]

Scott quotes at length from Knox's stern account of the tale of this "whore". This restored context provides a challengingly different insight into Woolf's choice of female personae. These feminine vehicles are far from placid, obedient, and willing slaves – they have the potential to be "haynous", as Knox puts it.[11] Woolf, in this way, also plays up the other side of the myth of woman as vehicle, vessel, metaphorical space: "she" is both complacent virgin *and* dangerous whore, a force to be subdued and contained.

The same sort of tension can also be observed in that other feminized/feminizing metaphor (and one with which Mrs Ramsay identifies) – the tree. Of course, Mrs Ramsay can be trusted to identify with anything, since she has the alarming habit of becoming "the thing she looked at" (p. 73);

but it is interesting, nevertheless, that the two prominent examples of this tendency involve the lighthouse beam (p. 73) and trees.

> ... she thought, insensibly approving of the dignity of the trees' stillness, and now again of the superb upward rise (like the beak of a ship up a wave) of the elm branches as the wind raised them. (pp. 174–5)

This passage ends with Mrs Ramsay's thoughts on the continuity of all she values in the coming marriage between Paul and Minta. The sight of the trees clearly leads her to conclude that "Paul and Minta would carry it on when she was dead" (p. 176). Mrs Ramsay identifies herself with the tree as a natural and unifying sign of an old order *status quo*. The trees emanate a sense of fettered power in the same way that we see the female form pressed into literary/cultural service as a fettered threat. This tension is also present in the story of Mary Hamilton: as a namesake of the Holy Mother, Mary the child-murderer is more disturbing than Mary Magdalene. From these examples emerges a contradictory figure of woman as passive sexual object, commodified tool, and also instrument of threat.

Warner has traced the aesthetic construction of this feminine/izing vehicle to its roots in classical antiquity, and to the origins of the caryatid:

> The women [of Carya were] led away as captives, still dressed in all their finery, and "to ensure that they exhibited a permanent picture of slavery ... the architects of those times designed images of them specially placed to uphold a load".[12]

The legacy of this early architectural embodiment of female enslavement is the paradoxical complicity of women in the patriarchal order. As vanquished sexual objects they literally hold up patriarchal institutions. If Mrs Ramsay represents the beauty and allure of this role, then Mrs McNab, the charwoman of the novel's middle section, "Time Passes", reveals to us the actual labour involved. As Beauty and

Strength they are both respectively enslaved as aspects of the same figure.

In *A Room of One's Own* Woolf makes a similar observation with regard to women's status inside and outside art:

> Imaginatively she is of the highest importance; practically she is completely insignificant. She pervades poetry from cover to cover; she is all but absent from history. She dominates the lives of kings and conquerors in fiction; in fact she was the slave of any boy whose parents forced a ring upon her finger. Some of the most inspired words, some of the most profound thoughts in literature fall from her lips; in real life she could hardly read, could scarcely spell, and was the property of her husband.
>   . . . What one must do to bring her to life was to think poetically and prosaically at one and the same moment, thus keeping in touch with fact . . . but not losing sight of fiction either – that she is a vessel in which all sorts of spirits and forces are coursing and flashing perpetually. (pp. 66–7)

The only comforting thing for feminists about a caryatid is that it is quite obviously a piece of architecture – a man-made construction – which can therefore be dismantled or bulldozed away without compunction. The sinister thing about a tree, however, is that it appears to be natural. To pull down a tree is to go against nature, against the natural order of things. In pastoral poetry, a tradition Woolf draws on for *To the Lighthouse*,[13] the tree is the symbol of patronage – political and literary (if they must be distinguished) – and under its shade ("umbra"), pastoral figures have languished from Theocritus to the present. But when idyll turns to elegy, which is the main movement of *To the Lighthouse*, there is a pastoral tradition which signifies this fall with the felling of a tree and the loss of its "umbra". The cause of this shattered idyll is usually a storm. Petrarch's second Eclogue (lines 2–13, 19–21) stands as the origin of this tradition:

> For no day for many centuries had seen so great a calm in the groves: on all sides gentle sleep possessed full-

fed flocks and shepherds; some as they sang constructed wooden staffs, or leafy garlands, or fluent reed-pipes; *when a dark cloud obstructed the shining sun, and suddenly and without warning night descended on us; the sky shuddered with a terrible hailstorm; rain and wind contested and lightning descended through the cloud-fissures. Standing higher than the rest, deeply smitten by a thunderbolt, the cypress fell headlong, shaking the hills and the fields on impact* . . . Trembling in the great crash of its ruin, a crowd of shepherds took flight who had formerly through the long day sheltered in its secure shade.[14] (My italics)

Woolf's famous "down-pouring of immense darkness" at the beginning of "Time Passes" seems to echo the Petrarchan descent of night.[15] The disappearance of Lily's tree just as clearly parallels the demise of his cypress.

Woolf's subversive engagement with the pastoral "umbra" becomes an important area of investigation in connection with her Post-Impressionist technique,[16] so – as with the case of Mary Carmichael – I was delighted to discover that this too has special relevance for Woolf's Scottish setting in *To the Lighthouse*. As a voracious reader of Dr Johnson, Woolf was doubtless familiar with his famous remarks on Scotland's lack of trees:

> "A tree might be a show in Scotland as a horse in Venice . . . . It may be doubted whether before the Union any Lowlander between Edinburgh and England had ever set a tree."[17]

The context of these remarks – *Johnson's Journey to the Western Islands* – makes them all the more noteworthy with regard to Woolf's setting. Indeed, along with Boswell's *Journal of a Tour to the Hebrides*, Johnson's book provides a most stimulating point of intertextual reference for Woolf's novel. Recent scholarship has drawn out the significance of Johnson's attitude to Scotland and trees, and this has important implications for readings of *To the Lighthouse*.

Peter Womack, in *Improvement and Romance*,[18] does for the post-'45 Highlands what Marina Warner does for the female form – that is, he traces the processes involved in the construction of a myth. There are some well established parallels between these two myths (land and woman operating as reciprocal metaphors; marginality; otherness, and so on), but there is a particularly interesting overlap in their metaphorical use which Womack brings to our attention: the tree. In a specifically Scottish context, he opens up the ideological significance of trees for the landscape of Woolf's novel:

> Thus Burns's trees, so far from expressing nature's immanent productivity, are specifically the sign by which nature is assimilated to a cultural code of ownership and patronage.
> . . . Scotland's treelessness was after all a long-standing reproach, notoriously revived by Johnson . . . : planting was the privileged type of enlightened Highland estate management. Trees are the cultivated landlord's visible signature on the land, the means by which he at once acknowledges, enhances, and appropriates – in a word, improves – its virtue.
> . . . The manager of the land, then, is to supplement nature and, in the same gesture, to naturalise the supplement, skilfully effacing the traces of skill which mark the disjunction between subject and object. Forestry, with its secular timescale and "shagged" appearance, is the ideal medium for this slightly evasive *coup*. In the splendidly wooded glens of the Short Tour, Improvement achieved its most spectacular synthesis: it identified itself with the vital principle of that which was to be improved.[19]

I cannot help thinking that Mr Ramsay is adopting the same insidious imperialistic tactic when he is observed by his children bringing "his voice into tune with" the local boatman, and affecting a "little tinge of Scottish accent which came into his voice, making him seem like a peasant himself, as he questioned Macalister about the eleven ships that had been driven into the bay" (p. 254). Mrs Ramsay's good work with the poor also appears part of a similar project of "Improvement and Romance" – infiltration and domination.

Annabel Patterson, the translator of the Petrarch quoted above, in her book, *Pastoral and Ideology*, emphasizes the many ways in which the genre of Pastoral has itself been "naturalized" – that is, sanitized of specific historical and political readings. This tendency to think of pastoral (elegy) as decontextualized/decontextualizing makes for some unfortunate repercussions in readings of Woolf's work. If her engagement with the genre is recognized at all, it is not regarded as politically significant. In proper generic context, however, Woolf's handling of the tree motif reveals the politics of her aesthetics quite clearly. Womack underlines for us the political implications of a Highland location, and makes clear the parallels between the appropriation as metaphorical vehicle and mythologizing of the Highlands, and the same processes enacted upon the feminine. The tree is common to both these mythologizing manoeuvres: its destruction vital for retaliation against both.

We might conclude that the way in which the ruling English patriarchy mythologized and allegorized Scotland into subservience correlates with the way it was accustomed to treating its wives. From this point of view, Woolf's Hebridean setting is perfect for a novel seeking to explore and dismantle the values of the old order right at the heart of its metaphorical stronghold – the institution of marriage. A country forced kicking into union with its neighbour provides an appropriate backdrop against which to arrive at a woman's assertion of selfhood and her rejection of marriage.

The Critics

'Good criticism is subtly suggestive."
Virginia Woolf, "Charlotte Brontë"

My Violet, I'm so glad that you like some of The Lighthouse. People in the Hebrides are very angry. Is it Cornwall? I'm not as sure as you are.
Woolf to Violet Dickinson, 5th June 1927[20]

Violet Dickinson's act of transposition fits comfortably with the common critical attitude to Woolf's choice of setting: *To the Lighthouse* is an elegy which records Woolf's coming to terms with the death of her parents; Mr Ramsay is therefore Leslie Stephen, and Mrs Ramsay is Woolf's mother; Skye is really St Ives (the location of the Stephen family's summer retreat); and the eponymous lighthouse is in fact Godrevy lighthouse. Woolf's references to setting are then regarded as careless inaccuracies – as further evidence of her introspective, biographical, and feminine methods. We are thus persuaded to read *To the Lighthouse* as a vague, somewhat mystical meditation upon the highly personal events of her family life. If, however, we stop substituting Violet's phantom "St Ives" and "Cornwall" for the words "Skye" and "the Hebrides" whenever we refer to them or encounter them in *To the Lighthouse* we might arrive at very different interpretations.

Why are those "people in the Hebrides" so "very angry"? I have been unable to identify the irate Hebrideans mentioned by Woolf, but she possibly has one in mind when she writes to Vita Sackville-West shortly after the novel's publication: "An old creature writes to say that all my fauna and flora of the Hebrides is totally inaccurate. Dear me! what's to be done about it?"[21] Lord Olivier (ex-Governor of Jamaica and a Fabian Socialist) is mentioned in the same letter but not identified as the "old creature" in question, although Woolf's comment to Vanessa Bell a week later makes him a strong candidate:

> Lord Olivier writes that my horticulture and natural history is in every instance wrong: there are no rooks, elms, or dahlias in the Hebrides; my sparrows are wrong; so are my carnations: and it is impossible for women to die in childbirth in the 3rd month – He infers that Prue had a slip (which is common in the Hebrides) and was 9 months gone. This is the sort of thing that painters know nothing of.[22]

Lord Olivier was not a native Hebridean, which rules him out as a person "in the Hebrides" but he is certainly a keen (yet seriously mistaken) defender of local detail.

Reviews of Woolf's earlier works testify to her already established reputation for factual inaccuracy.[23] Joan Bennett is one of the earliest critics to suggest that Woolf's apparent slovenliness in such matters might be gender-linked and of central importance to her style:

> Possibly Virginia Woolf's own inaccuracy in matters of fact is due to the essential feminineness of her mind. Or perhaps it is a deliberate carelessness about all that is not essential to her vision. It has been pointed out that her flowers bloom at impossible times and in impossible places; that her champagne bottles can be opened with corkscrews; that Claridges stands where no Londoner has ever found it. Those whom these vagaries leave unmoved, may wince when Orlando reads Sir Thomas Browne in the reign of Queen Elizabeth, or when Mrs Dalloway admires the character of Clytemnestra in the *Antigone*. Virginia Woolf is indifferent to fact.[24]

We are not, then, to credit Woolf with precision, however "deliberate" her "carelessness". Yet surely we should not charge Woolf with her own character's sin of literary slackness. But not only does she suffer the ignominy of being likened to the poorly read and ill-informed Mrs Dalloway, she is also accorded the muddled thinking of Mrs Ramsay: "First of all, at its best, [the feminine mind] has a special honesty, an honesty which comes of self-knowledge, and the power of distinguishing the essential from the accidental. Mrs Ramsay is more honest than her husband".[25] Woolf, then, along with Mrs Ramsay, is capable of reaching highly subjective and introspective truths – she does not trouble herself with mere facts.

The warmth of critical regard for such studied vagueness pervades most commentaries on *To the Lighthouse*. For example, James Hafley observes that "the setting is at once precise and vague". He attributes Woolf's "notorious lack of factual accuracy" to a higher concern for "artistic effect".[26] Woolf's failure to be exact is redeemed as a positive aesthetic device, a position which encourages a mystical reverence for Woolf's purported vagueness, and a dizzying resistance to dispelling it.

David Daiches, referring to Woolf's location as "an island

unparticularized and remote", remains convinced that the
Scottish setting is of no importance: "We know, from one
fleeting reference, that we are on an island in the Hebrides
but this is all the information we get."[27] His footnote is worthy
of the "old creature" and Lord Olivier themselves (if indeed
they be two):

> There are precisely three indications of the locality of the
> setting in TL . . . . And when Minta loses her brooch,
> Paul resolves that if he could not find it he would go to
> Edinburgh and buy her another. *Glasgow, however, and not
> Edinburgh would be the obvious city to go to if they were anywhere
> in the Hebrides, so this reference is misleading.*[28] (My italics)

This approach sits uneasily with Daiches's earlier
allusions to the symbolism of Woolf's "luminous halo" as her
"most adequate symbol of life",[29] and results in a bizarrely
bifocal critical lens through which Woolf's landscape is sur-
veyed. Either we see it diffusely as a remote, abstract, and yet
luminous blur; or we scrutinize it myopically for fidelity to an
Ordnance Survey map. Daiches draws his authority from a
blithely disclosed local knowledge.

> The present writer, who knows the west coast of Scotland,
> has amused himself by trying to pin down the island, but
> has found it impossible to do so. . . . What island in the
> Hebrides is there, large enough to contain a "town"
> (p. 21 etc.), yet small enough to appear "very small",
> "like a thin leaf", when one has sailed only a few miles
> away; possessing both cliffs, "park-like prospects", trees,
> sandy beach, sand dunes (p. 109), accommodating at
> walking distance from the "town" a large house with
> lawn, cultivated garden, tennis court, and other ameni-
> ties, *and with local inhabitants named McNab (the charwoman)
> and Macalister (the boatman). Neither Macalister nor McNab is
> an Island name.* VW's scene is either a composite one
> (with perhaps some suggestions from Cornwall) or largely
> imaginary.[30] (My italics)

Daiches has something of a blind spot when it comes to the

Isle of Skye, which is mentioned in the opening pages of the
novel and which meets many of the descriptive points he raises
here.

The "old creature" school of readers do at least acknowledge the novel's Hebridean setting, however quickly they
dismiss its relevance. More recent criticism follows Violet
Dickinson's equation of Skye with Cornwall, and holds with
Jean O. Love's endorsement of the novel as "frankly biographical".[31] Taking our cue from where, in *Moments of Being*,
Woolf gives her own retrospective assessment of the novel as
an act of exorcism – "when it was written, I ceased to be
obsessed by my mother. I no longer hear her voice; I do
not see her."[32] – we are encouraged to approach the work
psychoanalytically. But this sort of approach, when adopted
exclusively, abstracts the human relationships of the novel
from any specific setting. Typical of this tendency is Sue Roe
who describes the setting as "a potent atmosphere in which
to explore Lily Briscoe's potential as an artist, and in which to
demonstrate the highly complex, highly individual conditions
attendant on the artistic process, and its grounding in sexuality."[33] Acknowledgement of Woolf's Scottish setting would
support Roe's observations about the gender implications of
aesthetics at work in *To the Lighthouse*, but this possibility is
erased by her predominantly biographical interpretation.

Before turning to the particular connections I want to
make for Woolf's setting, it is perhaps worth acknowledging
that the general critical disregard for this issue incurs a greater
loss than mere factual correctives. Woolf's status as a modernist writer is also affected. M.H. Levenson, for example, puts
the case against Woolf's "luminous halo" in the context of
Ezra Pound's essay "The Hard and the Soft in French
Poetry":

> All of these metaphors imply an art that rejects precise
> statement and moral certainty in favour of the suggestive-
> ness and imprecision usually associated with symbolism
> or Impressionism. Pound, on the other hand, opposed all
> "mushy technique" and "emotional slither", preferring
> a poetry "as much like granite as it could possibly be".[34]

But if we begin to read Woolf's Hebridean references more precisely we might be forced to grant her metaphors, her imagery, her insights, her politics, and her aesthetics, a less sloppy repute. Once specific connections are acknowledged, we can see that *To the Lighthouse* has in its Hebridean location a sophisticated set of allusions which ground the feminist import of the work in a discourse of colonial metaphor. The appropriateness of Scotland as a parallel with woman in relation to ruling metaphors is ignored by the critical consensus, but must be addressed. Exploring the ramifications of this approach brings to light some connections which undermine orthodox views of Woolf's "notorious" imprecision.

Some Hebridean Connections

> "all seemed, after Edinburgh, so queer"
> Virginia Woolf, *Mrs Dalloway*[35]

Woolf's numerous Hebridean connections include: the events of the '45 – the story of Prince Charlie and Flora Macdonald; Johnson and Boswell's famous tour of the Hebrides; Sir Walter Scott; Milton's *Lycidas* and pastoral elegy;[36] *Macbeth*, and the *Iolaire* tragedy.

The last of these references is to the tragic loss on New Year's morning, 1919, of the Admiralty Yacht *Iolaire*. Over two hundred men returning from war service, most of whom were from Lewis, drowned within sight of their own homes and waiting families when the yacht sank, because of a confusion about the beacons, at the mouth to Stornaway harbour. The event was widely covered in the British press (in, for example, *The Times*, 3rd January 1919) and very possibly informs the references to shipwrecks in *To the Lighthouse*. It would certainly explain Woolf's reference to Stornaway as the novel's location during its composition: "I'm for the Isles of Stornaway." It also furnishes with a particular historical referent the passage in "Time Passes" which many regard as the novel's most abstract: "Did Nature supplement what man advanced? Did she complete what he began?" The passage follows "the silent apparition of an ashen-coloured ship" (pp. 207–8).[37]

In combination, these references form a cultural matrix of intertextual, factual, historical, and generic approaches to *To the Lighthouse*, and are themselves very much interrelated. Perhaps the most compelling connection is that of the '45 which in itself generates nearly all of the others. Johnson and Boswell were by no means the only literary pilgrims to the Hebrides, and their joy at sleeping under the roof which once harboured the Young Pretender has been shared by many – including Woolf herself – although her physical journey to Skye did not take place until very late in her life (1938).[38] She was, however, familiar with much of the literature of the Scottish Enlightenment and Scottish Romanticism, and grew up listening to her father reading – and rereading – all of the Waverley Novels.

With the figures of Mrs Ramsay and Mrs McNab ultimately in mind, I shall conclude with a brief look at how a reading of *To the Lighthouse* might be informed by consideration of the events of the '45. The story of the '45 rebellion and the Young Pretender's flight to Skye with the assistance of Flora Macdonald is so well known and so often recalled by popular imagination in connection with the island that it would be difficult *not* to invoke this myth with the mention of its name. But the following elements are worth emphasizing: the story of feminine accommodation and assistance to a retreating male hero (an aspect which includes the virtual erasure from most accounts of Flora's male assistant, McEachin, whose contribution to the adventure was at least equal to Flora's); a peripheral land, with mariolatric/Catholic associations, in rebellion against a central, London-based patriarchy; a Prince who cross-dresses as a serving woman to survive; the later appropriation of the whole story by the same London-based patriarchy for its consolation and entertainment. Woolf's novel is disruptive of this accepted myth in several ways. The Catholic mariolatric overtones of the Flora Macdonald myth seem in keeping with the allegorical power of Mrs Ramsay's maternal sanctity; and Flora's heroism seems in some ways in keeping with Lily Briscoe's own rebellion. The figure of masculine power dressed in a servant woman's clothes ("Betty Burke" – the Prince's alias) is not only useful in thinking about Woolf's concept of androgyny, but is also a graphic illustration of the feminine as the outward and allegorical, material and formal, to the masculine content of selfhood and sovereignty.

If we read *To the Lighthouse* in terms of the myth of the Young Pretender, we might well find some respect for Paul Rayley's choice of Edinburgh as the city in which to obtain a replacement brooch: Edinburgh was for Charles Edward the seat of power, it was and remains the access point for English power, and its castle is the home of the Scottish crown jewels. Although the Prince was welcomed by the citizens of Edinburgh, and instated at Holyrood Palace, he did not succeed in taking the castle. Minta's lost brooch and Paul's failure to find it or to replace it, then, broadly suggestive of a lost romantic quest, now take on specific historical inferences, not supplied by a critical preference for the appropriateness of Glasgow.

The story of the '45 also has some bearing upon the character of Mr Ramsay, the unfulfilled philosopher, who aspires to ultimate greatness and power but, recognizing his shortcomings, seeks refuge in feminine company, in retreat on Skye. He sees himself very much as a failed adventurer, the "leader of that forlorn party":

> Who shall blame him, if, so standing for a moment, he dwells upon *fame*, upon search parties, upon cairns raised by grateful followers over his bones? Finally, who shall blame the *leader of the doomed expedition*, if, having *adventured* to the uttermost, and used his strength wholly to the last ounce and fallen asleep not much caring if he wakes or not, he now perceives by some pricking in his toes that he lives, and does not on the whole object to live, *but requires sympathy, and whisky, and someone to tell the story of his suffering to at once*? Who shall blame him? Who will not rejoice when the hero puts his armour off, and halts by the window and gazes at his wife and son. (p. 60) (My italics)

As the "leader of a doomed expedition", a "hero" who "puts his armour off" reluctantly, old Ramsay has much in common with the Young Pretender. He is, after all, actually likened to "a king in exile" (p. 230) after the death of his wife. If we consider the earlier deferred and aborted attempts to reach the lighthouse, we might even find a new significance to the name of Ramsay's son – James was the first Pretender, Charles's father. We are further encouraged to think of the Ramsay children as royalty: "Cam the Wicked, James the Ruthless, Andrew the Just, Prue the Fair". (p. 39)[39]

Woolf's choice of other names must also be reconsidered. Daiches does not mention "Davie MacDonald", whose surname is not without some Hebridean significance and is of central importance to the '45, but he does assure us that "Neither Macalister nor McNab is an Island name." Yet both these names can be found in accounts of the '45, and more particularly concerning the events on Skye. When Flora and "Betty Burke" stayed overnight with Mrs Macdonald at Kingsburgh House, Mrs Macdonald's daughter and her husband Ranald Macallister of Skirnish were also guests there. It is recorded that Anne Macallister waited on the Prince at table, and that Mrs Macdonald:

> "*behoved to employ her daughter as handmaid to the Prince for putting on his women's cloaths.* 'For', said she, 'the deel a preen he could put in.' When Miss Macdonald (alias Mrs MacAllaster) was a dressing him, he was like to fall over laughing"[40] (My italics)

One of the main source books of material relating to the '45 is Bishop R. Forbes's *The Lyon in Mourning* whose title itself is echoed by Mr Ramsay's predicament in the final third of the novel: "he was like a lion seeking whom he could devour" (p. 241).

Forbes also rescues Mrs McNab. The hostelry at Portree where Flora Macdonald met with Bonnie Prince Charlie for the last time, was MacNab's Inn.[41] If we consult the holograph edition of the novel we also find that in draft form Woolf adopts the exact spelling of MacNab, which is altered for publication to McNab.[42] (The Royal Hotel now stands on the site of MacNab's Inn.) Mrs McNab emerges from this with a provoking genealogy: no one has doubted her status as charwoman (although Woolf's rendering of a Scottish working-class woman has been questioned), yet many have elevated her to the status of muse, chthonic goddess, "Nature" personified;[43] but now the particular historical significance of her name raises some important challenges to our political interpretations of her role. We must consider her, along with Mrs Ramsay, as the harbinger of a rebel, or as the slave of a failed patriarchal dreamer; we must consider her role in rescuing the Waverley novels (the main literary furniture of certain patriarchal households), and the possibility of her complicity with her own servitude. In introducing Mrs McNab, Woolf is confronting us with history, not concealing it.[44]

Mrs McNab also returns us to the gender implications of metaphor construction: in the traditional house of metaphor woman is the labourer, the mediator with the world, and man is the master. In *To the Lighthouse* Woolf offers an escape from these domestic duties. This alternative vision reflects the very real and enormous shift in women's status occurring in the first decades of the twentieth century. For if there is metaphorical housework to be done, then surely the point of Lily's final vision, when she draws the line down the centre of her painting, is to reject the old naturalized and feminized allegorical morphology – Mrs Ramsay and Mrs McNab – in favour of an obviously artificial construction which is made not out of, but by, a woman.

Crossing Divides: *Miss X, or the Wolf Woman*

Mary Orr

For Christine Crow

This essay offers the first critical reading of Christine Crow's *Miss X, or the Wolf Woman*, where a narrator looks back from old age at the growing pains of Mary Wolfe, schoolgirl, and reconstructs a novel surrounding Mary's relationships with her Classics teacher, Miss P, and her headmistress, Miss X. The novel makes two circuits, the first as Mary's *Miss X*, the second the narrator's version, *Miss X, or the Wolf Woman*. As yet, the novel has had few, rather lightweight reviews.[1] Most of these pick up the salient features of the text: its mass of literary references, its apparent lesbian confessional form, its perversities of narrative like the recurrent "X" ("seX", "eXtra", "SphinX-like", etc.). The novel is at once "élitist",[2] "anything but light entertainment",[3] "infuriatingly dense" and "too tightly woven".[4] What these reviews are actually pinpointing is the novel's *difference*, that all-too-familiar mode of relegation meted out to women and women's writing with all the concomitant evaluations of second-class status. It is precisely such assumptions and labels which *Miss X* questions. This then is the first point of divide, for if readers or critics expect familiar categories of plot and character, recognizable genre distinctions and an ending which restores their standpoint on fictional and sexual norms (even those of "lesbian" literature), they will find *Miss X* perplexing, abstruse, confusing or academic and theoretical. *Miss X* is racy and readable, as well as deliberately anti-canonical. It cannot thus have canonical criteria applied to it simplistically. Indeed, these reviewers are reacting in ways strangely similar to the critics of the French *Nouveau Roman* which appeared in the late fifties and early sixties, a genre which sought deliberately to break old habits of reading novels. Faced with Robbe-Grillet's and Butor's disorientating tactics, critics dismissed their work as élitist (because it was difficult to read) or tried to impose the old norms of coherence of character and plot, which yielded readings which are now laughable. If we are prepared to cross-examine our basic assumptions of reading, then *Miss X* is where we might start to escape from certain insularisms inherent in English writing. This essay will underline the 1992 "continentalisms" of *Miss X* where its Englishness (Mary Wolfe's schooling and Oxford education, symbols of the time-less bastion of liberal changelessness) is made part of a European Literary System, without bloodshed.

Recurrent motifs and word-clusters are what deconstruct and reconstruct *Miss X*. Readers unused to techniques which seem to thwart any monolinear, "what happens next", narrative thus need to pay particular attention to what follows so that the dynamic play of new meanings which these elements produce can be fully grasped. A key semantic field is that of sheep/goat references. Miss X is "goatish"; Mary is her "lamb". Miss X has a model goat called Capricorn; Mary buys her St X (Cross), a toy sheep.

The letter x disrupts the visual flow of the text as the word-clusters do on the semantic level. Each x used is upper case and often becomes a shorthand for the word "cross" or "Christ". Typefaces are frequently played with and readers are helped to locate significance when words or sentences are in bold type.

Names, too, form a nexus of meanings. The title of the novel automatically signals the presence of Freud: as well as the Wolf Man (male incest trauma) there is Dora (an hysteric incest trauma). I shall say more about these later. Other key names are those of the Egyptian pantheon, and in particular Isis and Osiris, and the nickname given to Miss X's paper-weight, a stone with a hole in it and known as Petrus Borel or "PB", initials which will stand for many things in the text.

The real Petrus Borel (Champavert) was a nineteenth-century poet and *lycanthrope*: that is, he suffered a madness which made him believe he was a wolf. Hence Borel links with Freud's case of the Wolf Man and with the ancient belief in were-wolves, those nocturnal metamorphoses of seemingly ordinary mortals. *Miss X* develops wolf imagery from all these elements, as we shall see.

Crucial to the text, then, is the question of how the self may be engendered if essentializing touchstones are displaced. Indeed, this novel could be seen as a fictional exploration of many questions on gender construction, some of them usefully raised by Judith Butler in *Gender Trouble*. In her introduction she asks, "Where and how do compulsory heterosexuality and phallogocentrism converge? Where are the points of breakage between them? How does language itself produce the fictive construction of 'sex' that supports these various regimes of power? Within a language of presumptive heterosexuality, what sorts of continuities are assumed to exist among sex, gender and desire? Are these terms discrete? What kinds of cultural practices produce subversive discontinuity and dissonance among sex, gender and desire and call into question their alleged relations?"[5] Some of the possible answers will emerge from the intersecting prongs of my study of *Miss X* which, because it sees the English novel from a context of continentalism as well, goes some way to reshaping the socio-political strains which lie at the heart of what makes novels "English". Such a "sexual/textual politics"[6] in *Miss X* will be the focus of my study, where I shall connect the dual meaning of the French word "genre" (gender and literary genre) to its project. I will show how *Miss X* challenges the fixed assumptions of "genre", by investigating first its generic hybridization, then the overarching mythic patterns which unify the text, the intertextual referencing and cross-referencing which pattern individual chapters and finally the "X" factor of the novel, the search for an unknown, but none the less identifiable, fictional entity.

The few critical reviews of *Miss X* to date have all been quick to contain and ghettoize it in generic terms. It has been labelled a "crypto-gothic fairytale, a semi-autobiographical account",[7] "a detective thriller/who dunnit; and . . . a coming out story".[8] While these elements are undoubtedly ingredients in its generic make-up, they are labels which, individually, stultify its polymorphous qualities. Again, like the French *Nouveau Roman*, which relied on the *pretence* of a detective story or the quest novel to engage reader desire in order to thwart it, *Miss X* sets up genre expectations only to dismantle them. Crow's novel is, however, taking this project beyond its continental forebear, particularly Robbe-Grillet's contribution. In the Seventh Piece or section, at the hinge, there is the cryptic reference to "Paranoid Jealousy and Obsessional FiXation" and "(*'jalousie*, a 'blind', Mary. Got your French notebook?'), the sadistic fantasies – *dismembered* women, in his case – of that weird 'New Novelist', Alain Robbe-Grillet, to name but a few" (p. 95). *La Jalousie* (meaning jealousy and a venetian blind through which a voyeuristic and obsessional husband looks) offers a model and anti-model for *Miss X*. On its deconstructive project for the Novel, Crow builds a reconstruction for Woman out of the pieces male writers have broken her into, like Osiris, but with no need, of course, of the piece Isis had to reconstitute by magic (see below). One of the aims of *Miss X, or the Wolf Woman* is the double reinstatement of the female subject into literature. Hence all the main protagonists are female and women-loving (not necessarily the same as lesbian). The book seeks to build up identikits of mystery women, where these can only be shifting approximations and not the scalpel-fine dissections they have undergone from knowing male writers like Henry James or Freud. The few men in the text are feminists like Mary's partner, Bill. This is where the Englishness of *Miss X* comes out and overpowers even the deliberately interchangeable cardboard cut-outs and gender stereotypes of Robbe-Grillet's French work. Specifically English characters (including male feminists) come back into play as culture and gender specific and, because they are complex in gender, seek a new *genre* identity.

It is where Crow complicates the conventional lesbian schoolgirl, coming-out novel that *Miss X* diverges from such English genres. This divide occurs at the fine line where Mary's friend, Annabel, a university lecturer in Gender Studies, offers a lesbian-feminist critique of Mary's novel, *Miss X*, but fails to encapsulate the novel in these terms (pp. 150–1).

Annabel's lesbianism, arguably the purist, politically separatist *modus vivendi* of Wittig, fails at the point of total woman-centredness. Mary's *Miss X* does perhaps, as Annabel claims, provide "a titillating trip for . . . salacious 'male' readers . . . oozing with the very concepts it purports to condemn" (p. 150–1). However Annabel cannot expect women writers like Mary to "develop our own New rhetoric, capable, since we must still fly in it, of hijacking the plane of Patriarchy from within" (p. 150) if she still operates on a simplifying "us and them" mode of genre definition. *Miss X* is feminocentric, a position which includes lesbianism and feminism but is not occluded by them. So what genre exists which crosses the divides women writers and the Wolf Woman experience, divides which are within and outside the canon? The mythic and intertextual dismantling and cloaking *Miss X* incorporates offers a way into this question and those posed earlier by Butler. Suffice it to say here, that it is helpful to put Crow's novel in the pending tray marked "Feminist anti-*Bildungsroman*", for it shows the engendering of the artist/creative voice via a metamorphosing, educational process, which has strong links with a kind of deconstructive, fictional autobiography.[9]

The mythic structures of *Miss X* are what disgorge its "X" factor, the sign of the unknown. They operate on three levels which I shall summarize briefly here before discussing them in greater detail later. The first is the Isis/Osiris myth which underpins the fourteen-part structure of the main text. This is a cumulative model, aligning individual elements, as if by metonymy. The second level mirrors the operations of metaphor and sets the engendering metaphors of *Miss X* against Biblical and Classical mythologies, the bedrock layers in Western Cultural formation on which layers of self-endorsing (phallogocentric) constructs are built. The third plane is what constitutes the overall frame of the novel, the Freudian, psychological/sexual theorization of self, best epitomized in the Oedipus complex. This can be seen to represent a derivative "scientific", applied mythic structure (mirrored by the strategy of intertextualizing myth, for example the use of Racine's *Phèdre*, to be examined later). Within the main text, the story of the Wolf Man picks up the story of the story of Mary Wolfe *not* told to her male psychoanalyst. Although all these mythic patterns are different (and I shall show how in due course), their overriding function in *Miss X* is their role as "authority" markers, the pegs upon which constructs of Self have been hung, constructs *Miss X* constantly undermines, often with wit and humour.

The Isis/Osiris myth, which accounts for the fourteen-piece structure of *Miss X* lies at the heart of Crow's subversive strategies. Chapters, in their traditional cause/effect linear and chronological chain, are replaced by "pieces", a patchwork of time, memory, flashback, flashforward stitched together. The putting together of these pieces by the reader is similar to what Isis had to do to her brother–husband's body. As myth, however, its paradigmatic structure allows a total requestioning of Woman as reader and writer.

> The great Mother Isis, solar disk and horns of a cow, who, in desperate mourning for her belovèd brother *and* husband Osiris . . . savagely slain and chopped up by their common brother, Seth, *loup-garou* if ever there was one, travels the world over to **find the fourteen scattered pieces of his mutilated body . . . in order to stitch them together again and turn Osiris back into a god**. (p. 66)

With delightful mock prudery, the identity of the fourteenth piece of Osiris's body, unrecovered because eaten by crabs, is concealed by Mary, yet revealed in the name of her R.E. teacher, Miss Prick. According to myth, it was Isis by her magic who replaced the original missing member. She was also the goddess who tricked Ra to reveal to her his secret name. The Isis/Osiris myth in *Miss X* puts power in the hands of Isis, by offering us a complete story without need of the phallus for its own symbolic to emerge.[10] Lacan's reworking of Freud and the cultural positioning of woman as the Other to men is thus also questioned if the status of the Phallus is decentralized. Instead of placing women on the side of lack (Freud, Lacan), *Miss X* emphasizes their completeness, or lack of need of the vital fourteenth piece for full self-expression (p. 77). With delicacy, the issue of what "lesbians" do is never made explicit simply because their gender wholeness as women takes precedence over sex. The passage in another tongue (French) from Monique Wittig's *Corps Lesbien* celebrates women's love and their answer to the fourteenth piece in The Fourteenth (and necessarily final) Piece of the novel (pp. 201–2). It therefore counterbalances Freud's interpretation of female sexuality and the girl's position within the Oedipus complex. Mary's ritual ripping apart of St X and Capricorn thus re-enacts the Isis myth by inverting it. She is deconstructing sheep and goat, heterosexual and lesbian codes in this scene, which has as its primal model a female Mother goddess. Mary thus fears that Miss X might castrate her not so much by cutting off her wolf's tail (p. 196) – she cannot be castrated for what she does not have/need anyway – but by cutting off her wolf's tale, the tongue to speak the whole event. Directly after the Wittig piece, Mary says she had "given tongue *a tergo* on another she-wolf's back". She has pieced together that Miss P and Miss X were lovers and given them voice. Miss X's secret name, given to us as early as page 131, is Philomela, but its implications remain unfulfilled until the end. Tereus, husband to Procne, tells her sister Philomela, with whom he has fallen in love, that Procne is dead. He then rapes Philomela and cuts her tongue out to silence her but Philomela *weaves a cloth* depicting what has happened. In the myths of Isis and Osiris, Philomela and Oedipus, what underlies their complexes is incest and castration. *Miss X* thus presents us with the older mother-myth of Isis, and her creativity in magicking up a missing phallus, as a worthy precursor of Freud and of a set of Classical mythological structures. And the number 14 appears twice in the text, in the vital date of the Oxford interview, in the city on the River Isis with Miss X and the New Tutor (pp. 64, 213), the feast of St Valentine, Lupercus and lovers' day.

The Biblical and Classical grand narratives which underpin *Miss X* are largely sheep and goat stories told from their two different perspectives. The Bible references always embody moral judgements, and separate groups into two camps. Mary remembers Miss P's reading of Matthew 25 – Christ separating the sheep from the goats – while she is sharing the rug with Miss X at Dungeness (p. 35 and Matt. 25:31–3, New International Version). Mary's guilt complex is at a critical turning point here, for while she judges the situation, she sides positively with the goats, whereas a conservative reader will judge both women negatively against the sheep. After the disclosure of the affair between a schoolgirl, Amanda Carbuckle, and the Maths and Chemistry teacher, Miss Hilbert, and their dismissal, the second lesson is read by Miss X. This time it is from the Old Testament, from Leviticus 16, and describes the sending of the scapegoat into the wilderness (*Miss X*, p. 84, Lev. 16:8–10). It is quite clear from the preface to this reading, Miss X is "struggling on manfully with the Abominations of Leviticus" that this is *man-orientated* judgement, utterly dépassé. Her harsh treatment of her colleague's lesbian affair scapegoats Miss X's own behaviour without atoning for it. Atonement is set up as a false category within *Miss X*. Amanda Carbuckle reappears as Ms Car, the new headmistress, in her old headmistress's office at the end of the novel. It will be the Reader in the text who will reinstate ostracism: "**You** who alone stigmatise, eXtirpate, erase, omit . . . the Other, the different, that which 'pollutes'" (p. 228). The purifying ritual does, however, occur, but it purges Levitical law itself, and arguably Miss X's double standards concerning it. This happens in the Eleventh Piece, that crucial cornfield episode where Mary separates *herself* from sheep/goat categories and concomitantly from the inherently feminist/heterosexist and lesbian readings she has had imposed upon her by her sister, Pin, and by Annabel. Mary re-ritualizes scapegoating by "scapesheeping". She rips the limbs off first St X (the sheep) and then Capricorn (the goat) and thus disintegrates the hold of first Biblical and then Classical constructs of the sheep or goat self. It is worth noting that counter to Israelite or Pagan sacrifices, Mary's is bloodless, even though it uses animal atonement surrogates. The end of the Eleventh Piece operates as a final act of counter-transference against Leviticus by quoting the end of the ritual, the priest washing his clothes to return to the camp (*Miss X*, p. 162, Lev. 16:26). Mary has not returned from the wilderness to the camp, but crossed into her own new camp, outside religious sheep–goat dualisms (Christian or Classical), free to "**rave** like the ancient prophets (I'm thinking of the abominable book of Leviticus) against everything oppressive

and anti-blasphemous, yes, **anti**-blasphemous under the Sun"
(p. 227). As Wolf(ie), emerging out of her now obsolete sheep/
goat clothing, she not only challenges the old patriarchal order
and its morality, she also challenges blood sacrifices and blood
taboos. The passages chosen from Leviticus come immediately
after the laws of purification required after "discharges causing uncleanness"; emission of semen and menstruation, the
latter the more serious uncleanness which requires lengthier
claustration and ostracism from normal activities. As Woman
and Wolf, blood-letting a natural attribute of both, Mary
undoes the totem and the taboo, ironically absolving herself
by quoting Isaiah 1:18 subversively – her "sins" are as white
as wool (p. 197). However, she dresses this in the white *angora*
wool jumper she chooses to wear, not the sheep's wool of Miss
X's attire and famous tartan rug.

This last direct reference to the Great Book is linked to
the other Classical myth which operates not as moral imperative, but textual imperative, an Ariadne's thread *out* of the
labyrinthine text of Mary's "personal Odyssey" (p. 198). This
emphasizes the non-Christian, pagan myths, the side of the
goat, epitomized in the Dionysus myth, god of pine trees, wine
and revelry, who is played in the school production of *The
Bacchae* by Amanda Carbuckle. Miss X's totem animal is
Capricorn the goat (a present from Dora, we discover). He is
replaced by St X, the sheep Mary gives her, until Mary
eventually has possession of both, and rejects both by dismem-
bering their chains of significance.

All Classics are linked to Miss P, the Classics teacher.
The equivalent of the New Testament passage she introduces
(significantly on the morning of the "elopement" of Miss X
and Mary to Oxford) is Homer's *Odyssey*. The sheep passage
here is the story of the escape of Odysseus from the Cyclops's
cave (p. 58). By tying himself and his companions under the
bellies of sheep, and hoodwinking the Cyclops by saying his
name is Outis (no one) he insures that when the Cyclops calls
for help and says "no one has attacked me" the others fail to
help. The escape by sheep here separates Outis from the
Cyclops, and it is this which is reinterpreted in *Miss X* by
Mary lamb. Odysseus blinded the Cyclops with a pointed
tree trunk directly in his single eye to avenge the Cyclops's

cannibalism of his companions. At the very beginning of *Miss X*, Mary encounters the psychoanalyst, whose interest

> vanished at once behind those sinister dark glasses – more a visor than two separate lenses – bunched like *a single, blind eye in the middle of his forehead* . . . "And what is her name?" he proceeded . . . pencil poised rapaciously above the virgin page.
> "Miss X," I replied like a shot. (p. 1, my italics)

The psychoanalyst is the cannabalistic Cyclops about to transfer Odysseus's act of wounding by a pointed implement to Mary and her as yet blank case notes. Mary escapes his devouring question by the "Outis" argument. "No one", that is Miss X, is to blame, but this time there is a change of sexual and personalizing identity of the term. Outis is always Odysseus, the initial "O" linking the two directly and synonymously. "X" in *Miss X* is however a shifting and unstable label outside the clutch of phallogocentric analysis. By defying the Analyst/Cyclops, and the Outis/Odysseus one-to-one relationship with herself, Mary leaves Plato's Cave and the Psychoanalytic womb for feminist pastures new. This journey beyond male monofocalisms and blindness takes Mary also beyond the new Stations of her X: Miss X, Mrs X, Mary's OXford tutor, and Miss X's earlier unknown victim, **"this same Nobody in a flat in Paris behind the Musée de Cluny"** (p. 170), whose identity is eventually revealed or indeed concealed as Dora. Like Freud's famous (lesbian) patient who escaped her analyst's clutches, the name may in *Miss X* be a further pseudonym, the ultimate cloak for making public the private self. It is with Crow's Dora that the Odysseus connection is remade and appropriated for *woman* as hero (sic). It is in the Cluny museum that the mediaeval tapestry, "*La Dame à la Licorne*", is kept. The *licorne*, unicorn, has its sharp pointed instrument attached to its forehead at the place where the Cyclops has his eye. The French title for this famous tapestry denotes a Lady *with* a unicorn; the *à la* construction, however, also translates the English "unicorn woman", an interesting female variant of the centaur. This cross-dressing of man-animals of classical myth occurs not only in the case of Crow's *Dora*, but more importantly in her *Mary Wolfe*. Her personalized *Odyssey* reharmonizes "Outis" with the identity of an author at the end of the novel via the Actaeon story (p. 24). Actaeon was turned into a stag by Artemis because he saw her bathing naked; his hounds, failing to recognize their master's voice, turned on him and devoured him. Mary in the Fourteenth Piece, in stag's head uniform (horns on her head), stares in at Miss X's "naked pelt" from the tree outside Miss X's bedroom window (p. 196). She is in stag (drag) uniform (unicorn), but unpunished for this infringement of the other's nakedness, because both are the same sex. Five pages later, Mary Wolfe and Miss X "come out" because they are written and named by Mary on the school window which she revisits. Ironically, there is *no one* there to read it. She has now broken the last taboo (as Isis did with Ra) of naming the god (p. 201). Mary then dreams in her bed at the *Unicorn* Hotel of Miss X as the Wolf in *Little Red Riding Hood* entering the window (as in the Wolf Man's tale), not to devour, but to make love to her, Mary *Wolfe*. Hunter and hunted, lamb and wolf are not opposites, but two faces of the same entity. At the end of the novel the Actaeon myth and its reworking in Mary come together with Mary as Wolf and the story of the shepherd *boy* who cries wolf, "**Actaeon! Nobody! Miss X! Wolf! Wolf!**" (p. 227). When Mary cries wolf, though, she also takes on her own true identity instead of uttering the empty fictional one of her male predecessor.

The blinding of the Cyclops/Analyst is also the crossover point in *Miss X* to Freud's psychoanalytic reinterpretation of the Oedipus myth, and his case of the Wolf Man. Oedipus which means "swollen-footed" (his father Laius bound his feet together and ordered a shepherd to leave him on a mountain to die) fulfils the oracle which predicts that he will kill his father and marry his mother, by killing his father, solving the Sphinx's riddle, marrying his mother Jocasta, and causing her suicide, before blinding himself. In *Miss X*, the story repeatedly "psychoanalyses" Freud from the other side of the fence: the question is whether heterosexist assumptions implicit in the Oedipus complex are blind or have blindspots? One of the strategies of the novel is to subvert the most deep-

rooted models of phallogocentrism by caricature or animaliz-
ation. The gods turned humans and themselves into animals
for purposes of disguise or punishment. Freud, in *Miss X*, is
turned into the German dachshund bitch, Sigmund, who suffers false pregnancies, fears water and can "sometimes be
temporarily roused from congenital depression and/or hysteri-
cal, self-defensive anXiety – incipient agoraphobia in her case,
perhaps?" (p. 35). However, such blatant caricature, though
humorous, is not simplistic concerning deep psychological
investigation. It suggests more complex structures are
required, particularly for Woman, than Freud allowed. This
is suggested first by the reworking of the Oedipus myth itself:
Miss X suffers swollen feet; Mrs X or the power of the mother
replaces the patriarchal domination in Freud (see the important fantasy scene of the "murder" by language of the mother
in the kitchen, pp. 170–4). At the end of the novel, there is
the case of the Wolf Man, given as the epigraph to the crucial
Fourteenth Piece and to the novel itself. True crossing over
the divide of personhood or identity is at stake here, prefigured
at the crucial turning point at the end of the Seventh Piece,
where Mary's dreams turn her into Miss X looking at Miss
P.

In the Fourteenth Piece, the metamorphosis transforms
the wolf man into wolf woman, literally. The text gives a
potted account of the boy's version of seeing six or seven
wolves on the branches of a walnut tree outside his bedroom
window, and quotes Freud's belief that the boy had subli-
mated the "repressed wish to copulate with . . . his own poor
father – a wish that succumbed to repression and re-appeared
as phobia because of its unacceptable implications: *Castration
and Femininity* (sic, sic, sic)!" (p. 197). The response Mary as
Wolfe has is different, for, having overcome various taboos in
the course of self analyses, and not being a boy suffering
castration anxiety in the same way (that missing fourteenth
piece) she *is* the wolf in the tree outside the Pagoda staring
in at Miss X naked like Artemis before Actaeon (p. 196). The
reference to the "stag's-head uniform" and Miss X's "pelt"
also link the two women to the other mythological wolf men,
werewolves. However, because both women share lupercalian
characteristics, they *are* wolves. Furthermore, the wolf is not

the object of terror (as in the Wolf Man case) but the subject relating to another subject, equally "castrated". As wolf looking in, not being looked at, she is also the *subject* of the gaze, not its object (the so-called female position).

The more interesting layer of psychoanalysis is not inverted in the same way, but explored from the Other point of view. It is the theorizing of the Oedipus complex in terms of Art beyond the stereotypes of sex and gender. This is signalled in the epigraph to the Eleventh Piece, from *Totem and Taboo*: "In Greek tragedy the special subject-matter of the performance was the sufferings of the Divine Goat, Dionysus, and the lamentations of the goats who were his followers. . . . I should like to insist that its outcome shows that the beginnings of religion, morals, society and art converge in the Oedipus compleX" (p. 143). This is where Butler's questions re-emerge, and from the point of view of *Miss X* are placed centre-stage by the post-Freudian response from Annabel who "interprets" *Miss X* and its author, Mary Wolfe, under the nickname "Wolfie" for us as if both were on her couch (pp. 150–1). Yet the excess of her style only questions to a double degree the edifice the whole psychoanalytic project is built upon, a questioning with no clear directions to answers until the final analysis the *reader* gives to the story of *Miss X, or the Wolf Woman*. The speaking forth (defying the castration of woman's tongue) as in analysis is the point at which the frame (the visit to the psychoanalyst which begins and ends the novel) and its contents (the Fourteen Pieces) at once meet and diverge.

The properly intertextual dimension in the pieces of *Miss X* cross-examines the use of cross-references from the "Great InterteXtual Literary Storehouse of the Past" (p. 79). The many intertexts take up at the micro level the challenges to genre constructs of mythology examined above at the macro level of *Miss X*. Butler's questions concerning the kinds of cultural practices which produce subversive discontinuity and dissonance among sex, gender and desire and call into question their alleged relations puts in a nutshell the problem women writers have in creating a properly Woman genre. Cultural heritage is male constructed and valorized, so any borrowing therefrom is inherently operating against that aspect of the Woman project which desires a separatist stance. Is a feminist intertextuality then possible or something only lesbian writers can establish as a tradition? Theirs is, after all, where subversive discontinuity and dissonance resounds clearest. (This position is not wholly new but follows in the footsteps of homosexual male writing which subverts bourgeois, heterosexist forms.) Or are women writers now in the process of creating their own storehouse? The steps Mary is made to undergo offer, I believe, a way through this battlefield and I want to stress the positive nature of fencing with "male" literature, for it is a formative training ground from which Woman self can emerge perhaps with more differentiation potential than men can muster. The trauma of sons attempting to break free from the influence of their "strong" poet fathers, described in Harold Bloom's *The Anxiety of Influence*, simply does not apply.[11]

The male French writers, whom Miss X and then the New Tutor at Oxford present as reading lists for Mary, provide her with foils and models which are doubly other. Their Continentalisms, and foreignness, highlight Mary's own cultural roots, first by contrast with Racine (which means a root) and the tragedy of incest *Phèdre* (another Miss *P*!) epitomizes. This is the interlocutor intertext between the Classics and the Moderns, Greek tragedy and Freud's investigations of the subject in *Totem and Taboo*. Racine launches Mary out "entre chien et loup" (into the twilight) to the cluster of nineteenth- and twentieth-century French male writers whose intertexts offer a French parallel to the sheep/goat grand narratives, a toss-up (like that of Pascal's wager, p. 38) which gives an illusion of choice. Daudet's *La Chèvre de Monsieur Seguin*, Blanchette, and *Le Petit Prince* by St Exupéry (Xupéry) are minor works (p. 33). Their noteworthiness is that Miss X is fond of them despite their low literary status, that is, she offers Mary double-standard texts here. Only Baudelaire's *Fleurs du Mal* has the necessary strength to force out the subversive, genuine nature Miss X embodies: her perversity in splintering relationships (like the poet observer who wilfully destroys a glazier's wares and laughs at the damage he has done in *Les Poèmes en Prose* referred to on page 169); her lesbianism and the paradoxical censored speech she allows Mary to utter. It is however, the decadent, erotic and forbidden (taboo) frankness of love and passion which Baudelaire's poetry releases in Mary, the discussion of which with Miss X elicits the oblique confession of love between them. Here it is the heterosexual love poetry, the first line of "La Chevelure" – "O toison, moutonnant jusque sur l'encolure" and the chorus and final line from "L'Invitation au Voyage" – "Luxe, calme et volupté" (p. 37) which acts as a medium for the crucial condemned pieces which discuss lesbian love: first a line from "Lesbos" – "Car Lesbos entre tous m'a choisi sur la terre" (p. 69) with its *male narrator* and then "Femmes Damnées", the last stanza of which is the epigraph to the Sixth Piece and shifts focus to the wolf status of such women. (For non-specialists in French, a paraphrase of the stanza is given on page 21 and page 187 of the novel). It is in the reading of "Lesbos" that Mary labels Miss X's, and hence her own, sexual identity. It is from this point that Mary enters the stage of putting her female narrative voice-over on this stanza by becoming and speaking as wolf. It is a journey beyond Baudelaire's to new territories suggested by the last line in the last poem of *Les Fleurs du Mal* (and directly before the "Pièces condamnées"), "Le Voyage" – "Au fond de L'Inconnu pour trouver du Nouveau!" (p. 144), but one equally open to reader censorship. Baudelaire opened his collection with a challenge to the hypocritical and judgemental reader: "Hypocrite lecteur, – mon semblable, – mon frère", which Mary as wolf opens up, re-genders and personalizes at the end of *Miss X*: "Friends, Chickens, Citizens, Sheep, Goats, Children, Readers, Hypocrites, Writers, Lovers, male *and* female, Patriarchs, beware my gentle, padding footsteps . . . " (p. 227). By learning to speak for the pain of condemnation, marginality and ostracism (the "Femmes Damnées" and Vigny's dead and mute he-wolf, "La mort du loup", p. 127) in her own voice, that howl of release on page 229, a crying wolf because she is one, Mary thus defines her own genre beyond Baudelaire and beyond male homosexual French authors such as Gide and Proust. They serve as foils, and foreign others to her proper English femino-lesbian self, so that she understands better her own cultural position in an utterly English writing context.

The strands of English references emphasize two stages

of mediation in Mary's self-expression. The first is represented
by Webster's *The Duchess of Malfi*, a murder play like *Phèdre*
but a rumbustious link*man* to wolf texts (the epigraph to the
second half of *Miss X*, page 105). It shares with Radclyffe
Hall's *The Well of Loneliness* a necessary but temporary resting
place of emptying – the wolf finding her grave, and the lesbian
vale of tears – before new embodiment can occur. Like Miss
X, these writers offer first generation models of wolfhood and
lesbianism (Mary assumes Radclyffe is a male name at first,
page 46), still subject to double standards and stringent censorship. The cross-over point is Virginia *Woolf*, Mary's sexual,
cultural and literary/stylistic older sister. The topos of the
lighthouse protrudes throughout *Miss X* as a rock/touchstone
for the developing writer. First it is a prophetic metaphor, an
oracle to be fulfilled, "decadent and erotic as the very song of
the Sirens . . . my Rock, my Resting-place, my Lighthouse
Tower" (p. 26): then the actual site of desire, "across the
sheep-dotted *dykelands* to Dungeness, there to besport ourselves
at the foot of the old lighthouse – now *there's* a lone wolf for
you" (p. 34, my italic emphasizes the pun); it next metamorphoses, on page 38, into an image of waiting life and enlightenment "with the great, blind but somehow still watchful eye of
the lantern, waiting patiently until the twilight" (a positive
Cyclops remodelling). Virginia Woolf's *To the Lighthouse*,
Orlando, and the possibility of the Writer as Woman are intro-
duced on page 45 as tentative dawnings of Mary's awareness
just prior to the Oxford interview. That interview is the thresh-
old experience which unleashes the lesbian, the New Tutor,
and the torch of learning which becomes personalized as
"Imagination, heart of the intellect, the only sighted Lighthouse, the one true star . . . the Torch of Life itself, perhaps"
(p. 64). It is via literatures that Mary's authentic and then
imaginative, fictional life takes shape. The Woman novelist
has no further need of the Ivory Tower when she climbs her
own lighthouse one (p. 199). Woolf is therefore the queenpin
influence over Mary Wolfe, the hidden source, **"The other
Miss X. Imagination, Queen of moral Faculties** . . . The
Wolf in the desert whose same eyes (Gk. *homos*) you fear as
your life" (p. 232). This link is indeed suggested two pages
previously, and includes the tantalizing insertion of the same

name as that of author herself: "Actaeon! Miss X! Xtine Crow! Mary Wolfe, Woolf, Wolf!" (p. 229). The question is whether *Miss X* has indeed overcome this Good Big Woolf by its end or whether, like Mary's own *Miss X*, it is "simply some intoXicating ole lycanthropic pun" (p. 232), which, now exorcized, will allow Crow to develop a veritable Woman voice in no further need of *Wolf Woman*. Perhaps her next novel will demonstrate a post-Woolfian, but utterly Woolf-inspired voice.

By linking a writer-self to Mary via *Miss X*, the genre issue in both its senses is unified once more. While more questions than answers still exist concerning the real freedom of Woman's true expression outwith literary culture and its definitions of gender, *Miss X* none the less engenders the unknown, the uncharted voice of a woman becoming writer and how she engenders herself through engendering her (wol-fian) species of writing. In this personal quest for identity, which is at the same time not an autobiography, the novel identifies the need for a constant investigation of the problem-atics of genre to include, not exclude, the other/foreign as part of its project. Intertexts, myths and generic stereotypes like the "lesbian" novel *en abyme*[12] in the text thus make the Eng-lish, protean, feminocentrism of Crow's work more evident. Its boldness gathers strength visually (both metaphorically and literally, as the passages in bold type increase); its experi-mentation with cross-reference and cross-reading across cul-ture shows how breakage and Butler's call for practices of "subversive discontinuity" can be actualized. As deconstruc-tive fictional autobiography of an alternative, but very Eng-lish, second generation feminocentrist, *Miss X* crosses the div-ides between categories of gender and genre, and provides bridges into new territories. The novel points forward to further forays into the unknown. It is an intricately con-structed, contemporary **P**an-Dora's **B**oX, perhaps the real identity of the paperweight, Petrus Borel.

A Voice Between The Bars?

Christine Crow

"Cimetière Marin"
("Graveyard by the Sea")

"Ce toit tranquille . . . "
Paul Valéry, *Le Cimetière Marin*

"St Andrews by the Northern Sea
  A haunted town it is to me!"
Andrew Lang, *Almae Matres*

Tall, spindly towers between whose walls
A glimpse of ocean and of wheat,
Grey sentinels above the land,
The old Cathedral ruins stand:
St Andrews' "cimetière by the sea"!
Yes, this walled graveyard thick with tombs
Reminds me of Paul Valéry.
To this lone spot I climb to read
His famous poem on the dead.
Nor can I, though I strain and curse,
Keep back its echoes from my verse.
See how I use a shorter line
– eight and not ten that soars to twelve –
It's all in vain; the memories press,

While all about me as I write
His images seduce my sight:
The shimmering sea just like a roof,
The marble angels so aloof
And all the sculpted codes of death
– the scythe, the hour-glass and the skull,
The skeleton with Zeno's arrow –
That poets favour, ready-made,
As if to prove they have a trade
With masons, fleshers[1] and the rest.
(Is it to capture or erase,
This frenzied courtship of the page
That craves for immortality?).

Yet this famed graveyard in the North
(Marie de Guise was married here)
In many ways is not the same.
Here no dry cricket grates the air;
No shady pines pulsate in heat,
Stretching dark bars against the wheat.
No white-sailed yachts, but fishing smacks
To peck and scold the breezy main.
Here where John Knox once raged and foamed
And roused the jealous mob from Crail
To wreck the idols of the Pope,
Gold as the treasure-troves of hope,
The wind that howls is keenly toothèd
Against the snares of sun and sleep
– that braith which *ever* blasts the page –
And ne'er ripe fruit but thistles spike
The dreich[2] grey mist they call the "haar",
Creepin and crawlin everywhere.
The sting of salt, the gulls' shrill cries,
My "Cimetière marin" by the sea
Not that of old Paul Valéry!
No longer must I toe the line
And bleat of things *men* call divine,
But find a voice that's truly mine
And shouts my own live consciousness,

My *own* impatient doubts and fears,
Not his, beneath the ground in Sète,
The very graveyard of his poem.
(Yes you, Paul Valéry, my friend,
The *real* worm had you in the end!
Your consciousness, your tears, your pen,
All now surrendered to the clay
Which forms your wolfish marriage-bed.
Man is the measure of all things,
The pious doos,[3] the angel's wings.
All flees, as porous as the flesh,
Be it a brilliant Grecian blue
Or kilted like the rest of us.
My "charming breast" will bite the dust,
Just as you said all women must:
Our shining eyes, our teeth, our thighs
And what man lusts for all his life,
Confused, no doubt, with the unconscious).

Yet still, P.V., your phrase I hear,
Yoking my mouth to your lost ear,
Familiar though you are not here.
Here where the canny gods retreat
Like tortoises inside their shells
And golfers' tombs compete with lairds'
Amongst the croaking rooks and crows,
Where wings the cormorant or shag
Across the thrawn, tumultuous deep,
And where white horses – not just sheep –
Prance round the gravestones at my feet,
Exiled myself in Scottish clime,
I am the worm who turns for thee,
The lion who lives on sheep devoured.
Out of the eater comes forth meat,
The gift of sweetness in the flowers.
Aye, where the bones of Ossian[4] chuckle,
And matrons reap their names in death
(Euphemia MacGregor as at birth),
And great Poseidon casts his nets

With a certain dour, ironic mirth,
The Auld Alliance[5] lingers yet!
Nor is it parody alone
That toils to bite the hand that fed:
I whose proud, infant lips were stung
Once in my cradle by a bee,
Just like St Ambrose, so they said,
And whose own personal snake and key
Is passion for analogy.
Amongst the tombs, the towers, the wheat,
My severed head athwart Time's stream,
Cut off like Orpheus at the neck,
I sing to you o'er the abyss
And send you this deep mental tear,
Or if you like, this red, red rose,
Which some would simply call a kiss.
And, as the sun returns to paint
Its dazzling shadow on my book,
Beneath the ever changing clouds,
Hear your own silence haunting me,
So close within it is my own,
The same yet different, different yet
The same in its strange emptiness.
Thanks to the womb which gave us birth,
Hive of a thousand humming-bees,
Resplendent bitch, the Sea, the Sea,
Biting its ever sparkling tail,
Two "cimetières marins" North and South,
Sète and St Andrews, join in me . . .
That eye which needs *these* things to be,
Yet dreams it could be anywhere!

St Andrews, August 1989

Le Cimetière Marin (1920) is one of the great classics of European Literature and, true to Paul Valéry's interest in the workings of the human mind in its most general form, could be said to orchestrate, as they appear to flow through the consciousness of his first person speaker, the central philosophical commonplaces on which European thought is based: mind and body, movement and permanence, appearance and reality, life and death.[6]

What would happen if the voice of such an "amateur d'abstractions" were allowed to reveal the hidden "repression of the feminine" which such philosophical discourse takes as its founding cultural metaphor[7] and which, with his own secretly subversive mechanisms always at the ready, Valéry himself might be said to have equated with the natural palimpsest of all truly self-aware poetic form?

Such a deconstructive procedure is now, of course, standard in feminist critical practice. In choosing verse form for my current contribution (and why not allow fiction and theory to mingle more openly?), I seemed to want to raise certain questions in this area without prematurely "resolving" them as I might have been tempted in a "straight" theoretical piece – indeed, to present them (in the form of *my* first person speaker) through the general theme of self-awakening emotion generated by the Great Works of the past and thus common to both male and female writer alike. While such a sleight of hand might thus persuade the reader more readily to adopt the conclusions of my critical perspective (such the "poetic" wiles traditionally associated with the culturally feminine!), it would also serve to demonstrate how a Great Text can be "opened" to plural readings, playing "openly" in turn on the kind of mimicry or "voice between the bars" which it is currently fashionable to attribute to the female subject position in the intertextual action of writing itself.

"Man is the measure of all things", wrote Valéry for example (quoting Pythagoras). In setting this characteristically philosophical line in a context where the speaker, "I", has already been differentiated in the poem from "men" in the gender-specific sense (and not simply by association with feminine authorial signature, I hasten to add), I hope to have created a necessary "duck and rabbit" effect[8] where the

Figure 1

generic term must now be read in both its would-be neutral sense *and* in the gender-specific sense normally hidden beneath the table-cloth with such tortuous results in the *his*tory of thought – a partiality in turn temporarily restored to false universal status in the ironic "kilted like the rest of us" a little later on. A teaspoon of Discourse Analysis allowed to infuse ordinary speech? Once such a verbal force-field is set going (and I recommend its satisfactions, at least to the writer), other images can begin to problematize themselves as well. The "severed head" of Orpheus traditionally associated with the (male) Poet, for instance. If the female is represented culturally as the "Other" of (male) language and in turn the missing "Body" from which the "rational" subject constructs itself as different, is the female artist logically required to sing with her torso when *her* head is metaphorically cut off at the neck (a form of castration from the realm of the symbolic[9] never far away from less metaphorical violence, as the title of the present volume so graphically reminds).

Need(less) to say this kind of deconstructive pressure on

the seams of language is not at all the same thing as attributing mere objectifying body speech as the necessary domain of the female subject. The point is ensured throughout my poem by "her" identification with the flow of voice which steers through all such shifting gender positions, keeping "her" close, please note, to the same emotion of creative "detachment" which primes the narrative line of the original *Le Cimetière Marin*. Indeed, it is this revised or revindicated generality which might be said ironically to be restored by the end of my piece where the Sea, the Sea (already feminine in French, but that's *another* sparkling story) is made to coincide with the metaphorical womb which both male *and* female cultural positions now share as common mythical "origin", this in turn becoming the "ouroboros" or snake eating its own tail (traditional image of permanence in change found here, together with the serpent entwined round the key, as Valéry's personal emblem of his favourite "special subject", thought reflexively aware of itself).

Universality after all?

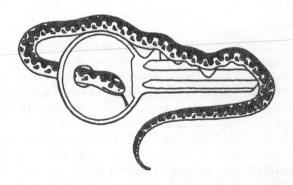

Figure 2

A heresy from the point of view of certain current feminist "orthodoxies", may be, but perhaps we risk putting *ourselves* in leg-irons if we deprive ourselves of access to that power of detached, creative invention which is by no means the sole prerogative of the male just because culturally conceptualized in falsely exclusive terms. I have tried to suggest something of the necessary hubris of the female artist's reclamation of this "lost" position by means of my narrator's self-comparison with St Ambrose (Ambroise was Valéry's own middle name as well as the saint whose lips were allegedly stung to inspiration by a bee – decidedly pre-Irigarayan[9] lips in his case, of course). I hope the multi-vocal context provided by the poem will convey at the same time the converse dangers to the individual self of sheltering from the rigorous tasks of such creative "emptiness" behind the politically general cloak: "the female artist has been suppressed, therefore I, female artist, have only to open my mouth to write a Great Work" (mine is *deliberately* not a Great Work, of course!).

Meanwhile what better palimpsestic space in which to set such intertextual bells ringing than a "graveyard by the sea" full of so many historical links between Scotland and France? With the help of *Tea and Leg-Irons* to amplify the chime of its communal message, I should like to think that the "Auld Alliance" in my poem can be made to symbolize a critical internationalism based on the potential alliance of male and female positions in prising open old texts in ever new ways, not the least their own hidden powers to subvert.

Fly away, dazzling pages, the speaker in Valéry's poem enjoins the book in which he reads, or, to the wave this time, dare to spring in a thousand pieces from the rock!

What if the "ouroboros" *is* a "male" trope? Daring to name our lions as well as our sheep, tolling the old to speak the new, why not harness its ancient power to celebrate our own "plural" writing too?

Figure 3

Notes

Caroline Gonda: Opening Remarks: pp. 6–14

1 Tobias Smollett, *The Expedition of Humphry Clinker*, 1771, frequently reprinted.
   (Letter from Jeremy Melford to Sir Watkyn Phillips, Bart., Oxon., dated Edinburgh, 18th July.)
2 Jane Marcus, *Art and Anger: Reading Like a Woman*, Ohio State University Press, Columbus, Ohio, 1988, pp. 225–6.

Dorothy Porter McMillan: Heroines and Writers: pp. 17–30

1 C.M. Grieve, *Contemporary Scottish Studies*, 1st series, Parsons, London, 1926, p. 42.
2 Lady Murray of Stanhope, *Memoirs of the Lives and Characters of the Right Honourable George Baillie of Jerviswood and of Lady Grisell Baillie*, Edinburgh, 1824, p. 33.
3 *Memoirs*, pp. 33–4.
4 *Memoirs*, pp. 36–7.
5 *Memoirs*, pp. 38–9.
6 *Memoirs*, p. 49.
7 I have taken the text of the song from Sarah Tytler and J.L. Watson, *The Songstresses of Scotland*, vol. 1, Strahan & Co., London, 1871. This admirable collection uses, I think properly, a more Scots orthography than *The Tea-Table Miscellany*. Ony gait, *anyway*; hing, *hang*; dowie, *dismally*; bing, *stack*; daundrin', *wandering*; dow, *has the strength to*; tykes, *dogs*; steeks, *shuts*.

8   Lady Grisell Baillie, *The Household Book of Lady Grisell Baillie
    1692–1733*; edited, with notes and introduction by Robin Scott-
    Moncrieff, Constable, for the Scottish History Society, 1911.

9   Joanna Baillie, *The Dramatic and Poetical Works*, Longman, London,
    1853, p. 709.

10 *Dramatic and Poetical Works*, pp. 758–9. Kirtled, *gowned* (a kirtle was
    a woman's dress).

11 I have taken the text of the song from Roger Lonsdale (editor),
    Eighteenth-Century Women Poets: An Oxford Anthology, Oxford University
    Press, Oxford, 1989, p. 265. Roger Lonsdale gives a full account of
    the publishing history of both poems. Gloaming, *dusk*; younkers,
    young people; bogle, *ghost* (the game is probably a kind of Hide and
    Seek); weded awae, *carried off by death* (the sense of "weeded out"
    still hovers).

12 *Eighteenth-Century Women Poets*, p. 263.

13 *Eighteenth-Century Women Poets*, p. 264.

14 Lady Anne Barnard, *South Africa a Century Ago: Letters Written from
    the Cape of Good Hope (1797–1801)*; edited with a memoir and brief
    notes by W.H. Wilkins, Smith & Elder, London, 1901, p. 31.

15 *South Africa a Century Ago*, pp. 130–31.

16 Quoted from Susan Ferrier, *Marriage*, 1818; edited with an
    introduction by Herbert Foltinek, Oxford University Press,
    Oxford, 1971, xiv.

17 *Sunshine and Shadow: Catalogue of the David Scott Collection of Victorian
    Paintings*, National Galleries of Scotland, Edinburgh, 1991, p. 24.

18 An early production, *The Quiet Heart*, (published in *Maga* December
    1853–May 1854; in book form in 1854), has a heroine who
    becomes a successful illustrator after breaking, albeit unwillingly,
    with her writer fiancé. There is an interesting reversal here of the
    respective activities of Mrs Oliphant and her husband who died in
    1859.

19 Mrs Margaret Oliphant, *Autobiography and Letters of Mrs M.O.W.
    Oliphant*, arranged and edited by Mrs Harry Coghill, Blackwood,
    Edinburgh and London, 1899; reprinted with an introduction by
    Q.D. Leavis, Leicester University Press, Leicester, 1974,
    pp. 127–8.

20 *Autobiography*, p. 128.

21 *Autobiography*, p. 150.

22 Janet Hamilton, "Oor Location", *Poems, Essays and Sketches*,
    memorial volume, Maclehose, Glasgow, 1880, p. 75. "Oor
    Location" first published 1868. Gey wheen, *good few*; drucken
    randies, *drunken, dissolute women*; rin the cutter, *to sneak drink into the
    house* (from evading the Revenue cutter, a ship employed by the
    customs authorities for the prevention of smuggling); fock, *folk*.

23 Tom Leonard, editor, *Radical Renfrew; Poetry from the French Revolution
    to the First World War*, Polygon Books, Edinburgh, 1990.

24   Marion Bernstein, "A Rule to Work Both Ways", *Radical Renfrew*, 298. "A Rule, etc." first published 1876.

25   Catherine Carswell, *The Camomile*, Chatto & Windus, London, 1922; reprinted by Virago Press, London, 1987, p. 154.

26   *The Camomile*, p. 305.

27   Catherine Carswell, *Lying Awake; An Unfinished Autobiography and Other Posthumous Papers*; edited and with an introduction by John Carswell, Secker & Warburg, London, 1950, pp. 115–16.

28   Willa Muir, *Women: An Inquiry*, The Hogarth Press, London, 1925, p. 7.

29   *Women: An Inquiry*, pp. 8–9.

30   *Women: An Inquiry*, p. 26.

31   *Women: An Inquiry*, p. 37.

32   *Women: An Inquiry*, p. 40.

Carol Anderson: Debateable Land: The Prose Work of Violet Jacob: pp. 31–44

This essay is a revised version of a paper originally given at the Second International Literature of Region and Nation Conference, University of Nottingham, 1988.

Definitions of Scots words are taken from *The Concise Scots Dictionary*, Editor in chief, Mairi Robinson, Aberdeen University Press, Aberdeen, second revised edition, 1985, and *Chambers Scots Dictionary*, W. & R. Chambers, Edinburgh, 1911, reprinted 1982.

1   Alan Bold, *Modern Scottish Literature*, Longman, London, 1983, p. 25.

2   For example, Isobel Murray, "The Forgotten Violet Jacob", in *Cencrastus* 13, 1983, p. 54; Janet Caird, "The Poetry of Violet Jacob and Helen B. Cruickshank", *Cencrastus* 19, 1984, pp. 32–4; Ronald Garden, "Violet Jacob in India", *Scottish Literary Journal* 13, no. 2, November 1986, pp. 48–64; Joy Hendry, "Twentieth-Century Women's Writing: The Nest of Singing Birds" in *The History of Scottish Literature*, vol. 4, edited by Cairns Craig, Aberdeen University Press, Aberdeen, 1987, pp. 291–309 (pp. 293–5); Douglas Gifford, "Myth, Parody and Dissociation; Scottish Fiction 1814–1914", in *The History of Scottish Literature*, vol. 3, Aberdeen University Press, Aberdeen, 1988, edited by Douglas Gifford, pp. 217–259 (pp. 242–3). There is also a brief but perceptive mention of Jacob by Susanne Ferguson in "Journeys of Understanding", *Cencrastus* 29, 1988, pp. 39–40.

3   *Flemington*, John Murray, London, 1911, edited by Carol Anderson, is to be republished by the Association for Scottish Literary Studies, probably in 1993. For a complete list of Jacob's major publications see the bibliography at the end of the essay (pages 43–4).

4 Hugh MacDiarmid (C.M. Grieve), "Violet Jacob", appeared originally in *The Scottish Educational Journal*, 17th July 1925, and is reprinted in *Contemporary Scottish Studies*, Scottish Educational Journals, Edinburgh, 1976, pp. 8–10; all references are to this later edition.

5 Anonymous review titled "Contes d'Ecosse" in *Journal de Secième*, 26th March 1923.

6 *Tales of My Own Country*, John Murray, London, 1922, p. 16.

7 Various contemporary critics made comparisons with writers such as Hardy.

8 Francis Russell Hart, "Scott and the Idea of Adventure", in *Sir Walter Scott: The Long Forgotten Melody*, edited by Alan Bold, Vision, and Barnes and Noble, London and Totowa, New Jersey, 1983, pp. 167–93 (p. 178).

9 Alexander Welsh, *The Hero of the Waverley Novels*, Atheneum, New York, 1968, p. 99–100.

10 In *The Other Voice: Scottish Women's Writing Since 1808*, edited by Moira Burgess, Polygon, Edinburgh, 1987, pp. 123–39. All references here are, however, to the first edition of *Tales of My Own Country*.

11 Trevor Royle, *The Macmillan Companion to Scottish Literature*, Macmillan, London, 1983, p. 152.

12 *The Lum Hat and Other Stories: Last Tales of Violet Jacob*, edited by Ronald Garden, Aberdeen University Press, Aberdeen, 1982. Further references are to this edition.

13 *The Fortune Hunters*, John Murray, London, p. 327. Subsequent references are to the same edition.

14 Margaret Atwood, *Second Words: Selected Critical Prose*, Anansi, Toronto, 1982, p. 282.

Margaret Elphinstone: Contemporary Feminist Fantasy in the Scottish Literary Tradition: pp. 45–59

1 Lewis Carroll, *Alice in Wonderland*, London, 1865.

2 Jen Green and Sarah Lefanu, *Despatches from the Frontiers of the Female Mind*, The Women's Press, London, 1985.

3 Margaret Elphinstone, *The Incomer*, The Women's Press, London, 1987.

4 Margaret Elphinstone, *A Sparrow's Flight*, Polygon Books, Edinburgh, 1989.

5 George Macdonald, *The Princess and the Goblin*, London, 1872.

6 James Hogg, *The Three Perils of Man*, Edinburgh, 1822; Scottish Academic Press, Edinburgh, 1989.

7 John Galt, *Ringan Gilhaize*, Edinburgh, 1823; Scottish Academic Press, Edinburgh, 1984.

8   Janice Galloway, *The Trick is to Keep Breathing*, Polygon Books, Edinburgh, 1989.

9   Sian Hayton, *Cells of Knowledge*, Polygon Books, Edinburgh, 1989 and New Amsterdam Books, New York, 1990.

10   Gregory Smith, *Scottish Literature*, Macmillan, London, 1919.

11   David Buchan, *A Scottish Ballad Book*, Routledge & Kegan Paul, London and Boston, 1973.

12   Sir Walter Scott, *Redgauntlet*, Edinburgh, 1824; Oxford University Press, 1985.

13   James Hogg, *The Private Memoirs and Confessions of a Justified Sinner*, Edinburgh, 1824; Penguin Books, London, 1986.

14   Robert Louis Stevenson, *The Strange Case of Dr. Jekyll and Mr. Hyde*, London, 1886.

15   Liz Lochhead, *"Mary Queen of Scots Got Her Head Chopped Off" and "Dracula"*, Penguin Books, London, 1989.

16   Emma Tennant, *Two Women of London: The Strange Case of Ms Jekyll and Mrs Hyde*, Faber & Faber, London and Boston, 1989.

17   Emma Tennant, *The Bad Sister*, Faber & Faber, London and Boston, 1978; 1989.

18   Naomi Mitchison, *Memoirs of a Spacewoman*, Jonathan Cape, London, 1962; The Women's Press, London, 1985.

19   Naomi Mitchison, *The Bull Calves*, Jonathan Cape, London, 1947; Richard Drew Publishing, Glasgow, 1985.

20   Alan Bold, *Muriel Spark*, Methuen, London, 1986.

21   Muriel Spark, *Symposium*, Constable, London, 1990.

22   Muriel Spark, *The Comforters*, Macmillan, London, 1957; Penguin, London, 1987.

23   Muriel Spark, *Loitering with Intent*, Macmillan, London, 1981; Penguin, London, 1981.

24   Muriel Spark, *The Prime of Miss Jean Brodie*, Macmillan, London, 1961; Penguin, London, 1965.

25   Muriel Spark, *The Ballad of Peckham Rye*, Macmillan, London, 1960; Penguin, London, 1963.

Caroline Gonda: "Exactly Them Words": Histories of a Murderous Daughter: pp. 63–82

I am grateful to Margaret Doody for introducing me to the story of Mary Blandy and setting me on the trail, and to Clare Devine and Alison Hennegan for helpful comments.

1   The engraving, reproduced as the cover to this book, is the frontispiece of an anonymous pamphlet, *A Genuine Account of the most Horrid Parricide committed by Mary Blandy, Spinster, upon the Body of her Father Mr. Francis Blandy, Gent. Town-Clerk of Henley upon Thames, Oxfordshire . . . .*, Oxford: Printed and sold by C. Goddard, in the

High Street: And sold in London by R. Walker, in the Little Old Bailey, and by all the Booksellers and Pamphlet-sellers, 1751. Abbreviated in subsequent references to *Horrid Parricide*.

2 *The Tryal of Mary Blandy, Spinster; for the Murder of her Father, Francis Blandy, Gent. At the Assizes held at Oxford for the County of Oxford, on Saturday the 29th of February, 1752 . . . . Published by Permission of the Judges*, London: Printed for John and James Rivington, at the Bible and Crown, in St. Paul's Church-Yard, 1752; abbreviated in subsequent references to *Tryal*. See also *The Genuine Trial at Large of Mary Blandy, Spinster, for poisoning her late Father, Francis Blandy, Gent. Town-Clerk of Henley upon Thames, Oxfordshire, at the Assizes held at Oxford, for the County of Oxford, on Tuesday the third of March, 1752 . . . .*, Edinburgh, 1752 [no publisher given on title page].

3 *A Letter from a Clergyman to Miss Mary Blandy, Now a Prisoner in Oxford Castle; with her Answer thereto. As also Miss Blandy's own Narrative of the Crime for which She is Condemn'd to Die. The Original Copy of this Letter in Miss Blandy's own Hand-writing, for the Satisfaction of the Public, is left with the Publisher*, M. Cooper, London, 1752, p. 5. Abbreviated in subsequent references to *Narrative. Miss Mary Blandy's own Account of the Affair between her and Mr. Cranstoun, from the Commencement of their Acquaintance, in the Year 1746. To the Death of her Father, in August 1751. With all the Circumstances leading to that unhappy Event. To which is added, an Appendix, containing Copies of some Original Letters now in Possession of the Editor. Together with an exact Relation of her Behaviour, whilst under Sentence; and a Copy of the Declaration signed by herself, in the Presence of two Clergymen, two Days before her Execution. Published at her Dying Request*, A. Millar, London, 1752. *N.B. The Original Account, authenticated by Miss Blandy in a proper Manner, may be seen at the above A. Millar's*. Abbreviated in subsequent references to *Account*.

4 For a digest of documents relating to the case, see William Roughead's introduction to his *Trial of Mary Blandy*, Notable English Trials series, William Hodge, Edinburgh and London, 1914, pp. 1–55. In addition to the trial proceedings (London version), Roughead reprints a selection of documents and pamphlets on the Blandy case, including Mary's *Narrative* and *Account*; he also gives a useful bibliography of primary sources.

5 See Roughead, pp. 190–204.

6 Edward Topham, *Letters from Edinburgh; written in the years 1774 and 1775*, London, 1776; quoted in Norah Smith's essay, "Sexual Mores and Attitudes in Enlightenment Scotland", in *Sexuality in Eighteenth-Century Britain*, edited by Paul-Gabriel Boucé, Manchester University Press, Manchester, and Barnes & Noble, Totowa, New Jersey, 1982, p. 48.

7 I am grateful to Liz Wilson for explaining the intricacies of Scottish marriage law to me.

8   "Doctors' Commons" was the Association or College of Doctors of Civil Law in London. Its buildings not only provided chambers for its members, but also housed the ecclesiastical and Admiralty courts. Serjeants, according to the Oxford English Dictionary, were "a superior order of barristers (abolished in 1880) from which, until 1873, the Common Law judges were always chosen." Mr Serjeant Stevens of Doctors' Commons was, then, high up in his chosen profession and well versed at least in English marriage law, still very much the province of the ecclesiastical court.

9   *A Series of Letters between Mrs. Elizabeth Carter and Miss Catherine Talbot*, 4 vols, F.C. and J. Rivington, London, 1809, vol. II, p. 76. Letter dated 22nd April 1752.

10 *An Answer to Miss Blandy's narrative. In which All the Arguments she has advanc'd, in Justification of her Innocence, are fully refuted. And her Guilt clearly and undeniably prov'd*, W. Owen, London, 1752, pp. 15–16.

11 Quoted in Roughead, pp. 143–4. On Catherine Hayes, see the article by Margaret Anne Doody, "The Law, the Page, and the Body of Woman: Murder and Murderesses in the Age of Johnson", in *The Age of Johnson: A Scholarly Annual*, 1987, 1, pp. 127–60. Doody's article also discusses Blandy and Jeffries, and reproduces a slightly different version of the "tea and leg-irons" engraving, which does not show the unlocked tea-chest. Blandy, Jeffries and Hayes are also discussed in Lincoln B. Faller's *Turned to Account: The forms and functions of criminal biography in late seventeenth- and early eighteenth-century England*, Cambridge University Press, Cambridge, 1987, which makes the case for a reading public thoroughly versed in the literary codes and conventions of crime writing.

12 *The Genuine Trial of John Swan and Elizabeth Jeffreys, Spinster, for the Murder of her late Uncle Mr. Joseph Jeffreys of Walthamstow in Essex*, C. Corbett, London [1752], p. 4.

13 *The Gentleman's Magazine*, XXII, London, 1752, p. 125.

14 Ibid., pp. 125–6.

15 *The **** Packet Broke-open; or, a Letter from Miss Blandy in the Shades Below, to Capt. Cranstoun in his Exile Above*, M. Cooper, London, 1752, p. 6.

16 *Narrative*, p. 5.

17 A particularly hostile account is *A Candid Appeal to the Publick, Concerning the Case of the Late Miss Mary Blandy*, by "A Gentleman of Oxford", J. Gifford, London, 1752. Accounts concurring with Mary's critical view of her father include *Memoirs of the Life of William-Henry Cranstoun, Esq.*, London, 1752, and *The Secret History of Miss Blandy, from her first Appearance at Bath, to her Execution . . . Communicated to a Gentleman at Henley by some of her Domestics*, H. Williams, London, 1752. *Original Letters to and from Miss Blandy and C-C-*, S. Johnson, London, 1752, gives a sympathetic account of Mary's relationship with Mr Blandy, as does *The Case*

of Miss Blandy: consider'd as a Daughter, as a Gentlewoman, and a Christian . . . By an impartial hand, R. Baldwin, Oxford, 1752.

18 Joan Morgan, *The Hanging Wood*, Macdonald, London, 1950; reprinted as *Mary Blandy*, W.H. Allen, London, 1979. Morgan's book is excellent in recreating the atmosphere and setting of the Blandy case.

19 *The Fair Parricide. A Tragedy of Three Acts. Founded on a late melancholy Event*, T. Waller, London, 1752, pp. 14–15.

20 *The Letters of Horace Walpole, Fourth Earl of Orford*, edited by Peter Cunningham, revised and enlarged edition, 9 vols, Richard Bentley and Son, London, 1891, vol. II, p. 285. Title abbreviated subsequently to *Letters*.

21 See Walpole, *Letters*, vol. II, pp.259, 265, 279, 281, 285, 293–4.

22 William Dodd, *The Sisters; or the History of Lucy and Caroline Sanson, Entrusted to a false Friend*, 2 vols, London, 1754. I am grateful to Michael Kerrigan for making the connection between this novel and the Gunnings.

23 *The Gentleman's Magazine*, XXII, London, 1752, p. 189.

24 Ibid. Both Roughead and Doody comment ironically on Mary's appeal to decency.

25 For a discussion of these patterns in sentimental fiction and in heroic tragedy, see my article, "Sarah Scott and 'The Sweet Excess of Paternal Love'", in *Studies in English Literature, 1500–1900*, forthcoming Summer 1992. My Ph.D. thesis, "Fathers and Daughters in Novels from Eliza Haywood to Mary Brunton", University of Cambridge, 1991, looks at these familiar patterns and their significance in a wide range of texts.

26 Roughead, p. 98.

Flora Alexander, Celebration and Exorcism: The Daughter–Mother Relation in the Fiction of Alice Munro: pp. 83–95

1 Marianne Hirsch, *The Mother–Daughter Plot: Narrative, Psychoanalysis, Feminism*, Indiana University Press, Bloomington and Indianapolis, 1989, p. 10.

2 Adrienne Rich, *Of Woman Born: Motherhood as Experience and Institution*, W.W. Norton, New York, 1976, Virago Press, London, 1979, pp. 225–30.

3 Alice Munro, *The Progress of Love*, McClelland and Stewart, Toronto, 1986, reference to the paperback edition by Flamingo, Fontana, London, 1988, pp. 3–31.

4 *Lives of Girls and Women*, McGraw-Hill Ryerson, Toronto, 1971; references to, and quotations from, the Penguin edition, Harmondsworth, 1982; *Who Do You Think You Are?*, Macmillan,

Toronto, 1978, published in Britain and the USA as *The Beggar Maid: Stories of Flo and Rose*: references to the Penguin edition, Harmondsworth, 1980.

5   For work done in the 1960s and early 1970s which exposed weaknesses in conventional thinking about women, see, for example, Betty Friedan, *The Feminine Mystique*, W.W. Norton, New York, 1963, Penguin, Harmondsworth, 1965; Kate Millett, *Sexual Politics*, Doubleday, New York, 1970; Rupert Hart-Davis, London, 1971; Eva Figes, *Patriarchal Attitudes*, Macmillan, London, 1970; and Germaine Greer, *The Female Eunuch*, McGibbon & Kee, London, 1970.

6   See, for example, Chris Weedon, *Feminist Practice and Poststructuralist Theory*, Basil Blackwell, Oxford, 1987, pp. 55–73.

7   Kate Millett gives an account (*Sexual Politics*, Abacus edition, 1972, pp. 222–8) of unsound arguments about the different capacities of men and women which were given currency in the United States in a widely used college textbook, *Selected Studies in Marriage and the Family*, edited by R. Winch, R. McGinnis, and H. Barringer, Holt Rhinehart and Winston, New York, 1962. The centrality of Freud as an object of feminist scrutiny in the 1960s and early 1970s can be seen in Juliet Mitchell, *Psychoanalysis and Feminism*, Penguin, Harmondsworth, 1975, in which she defends Freud against attacks made on his thinking by Betty Friedan, Eva Figes, Germaine Greer, Shulamith Firestone, and Kate Millett (pp. 319–55).

8   See the interview with Munro in Geoff Hancock, *Canadian Writers at Work*, Oxford University Press, Toronto, 1987, p. 214.

9   "The Peace of Utrecht" is in *Dance of the Happy Shades*, Ryerson Press, Toronto, 1968: references are to the Penguin edition, Harmondsworth, 1983, pp. 190–210. The story was first published in *The Tamarack Review* in 1960. "The Ottawa Valley" is in *Something I've Been Meaning to Tell You*, McGraw-Hill Ryerson, Toronto, 1974: references are to the Penguin edition, Harmondsworth, 1985. Munro mentions her own mother's illness and death in connection with these stories; see Hancock, op. cit., p. 215.

10 In *Friend of my Youth*, McClelland and Stewart, Toronto, and Chatto & Windus, London, 1990, pp. 3–26.

Valerie Allen: Making Myths and *The Merchant's Tale*: pp. 99–116

1   Frederick Engels, *The Origin of the Family, Private Property and the State*, first published in German 1884, first English translation 1902, frequently reprinted.

2   The fabliau is a type of short comic poem that flourished in France from the twelfth century onwards. Chaucer, writing in the late

fourteenth century, comes to it rather late. It is usually obscene, its plot tends to hinge on some elaborate deception, often sexual, and it is peopled with stock types – cuckolded old husbands and appetizing young wives. The humour is class-specific as well as gender-specific. Where courtly romance focuses on the nobility, the fabliau tends to feature tradesmen, urban dwellers, and sometimes the lower life of the Church – pardoners, mendicant orders, and clerks. Another point to keep in mind with regard to the anti-feminism of Chaucer's tale is that, as Richard Firth Green argues, Chaucer's court audience was mostly male; see his "Women in Chaucer's Audience", *Chaucer Review* 18, 1983, pp. 146–54. For further reading, see Janette Richardson, *Blameth Nat Me: A Study of Imagery in Chaucer's Fabliaux*, Mouton, The Hague, 1970, and Hope Phyllis Weissman, "Antifeminism and Chaucer's Chracterization of Women", in *Critical Essays on Chaucer's Canterbury Tales*, edited by Malcolm Andrew, Open University Press, Milton Keynes, 1991, pp. 111–25.

3 Throughout this essay, I refer to and quote from *The Riverside Chaucer*, edited by Larry Benson, Houghton Mifflin, Boston, Massachusetts, 1987. *The Merchant's Tale* occurs within the group of tales known as Fragment IV. My references will take the form IV + line number.

4 See *Rhetorica ad Herennium* (originally ascribed to Cicero (106–43 BC) and dating from the same period, edited and translated by Harry Caplan, Loeb Classical Texts, London and Cambridge, Massachusetts, 1954, pp. 22–5. For a discussion of feminism and mediaeval hermeneutics, see Carolyn Dinshaw, *Chaucer's Sexual Poetics*, Wisconsin University Press, Madison, Wisconsin, 1989.

5 It is a critical commonplace that the fabliau genre has its roots in realism and uses localized naturalistic setting. See Charles Muscatine, *The Old French Fabliaux*, Yale University Press, New Haven and London, 1986, p. 23, and Beryl Rowland, "What Chaucer Did to the Fabliau", *Studia Neophilologica*, 51, 1979, pp. 205–13.

6 *Middle English Dictionary*, edited by Hans Kurath and Sherman M. Kuhn, University of Michigan Press, Ann Arbor, 1956: "jangleresse = A talkative woman, nagging woman; also, a lying woman."

7 John Mirk (fl. 1403–?), *Festial: A Collection of Homilies: Part I*, edited by Theodor Erbe, Early English Text Society, New Series, 96, London, 1905, p. 230.

8 *The Thewis of Gudwomen (The Conduct of Good Women)*, in *Ratis Raving and Other Moral and Religious Pieces in Prose and Verse*, edited by J. Rawson Lumby, Early English Text Society, New York, 1969, lines 110–11.

9 *The Book of Margery Kempe*, edited by Sanford Brown Meech and

Emily Hope Allen, Early English Text Society, Old Series, 212, Oxford, 1940, pp. 130–1. Margery Kempe's dates are *c.* 1373–*c.* 1438; autobiography begun 1436.

10 See Aquinas, *Summa Theologiae* (composed 1265–74, unfinished at Aquinas's death), edited by Thomas Gilby et al., 61 vols, Blackfriars (in conjunction with Eyre and Spottiswoode, London, and McGraw-Hill, New York), Oxford, 1964–81; 1a 92 ad 1 (vol. XIII): "For the active power in the seed of the male tends to produce like itself, perfect in masculinity; but the procreation of a female is the result of the debility of the active power, of some unsuitability of the material, or of some change effected by external influences, like the south wind, for example, which is damp, as we are told by Aristotle."

11 Compare how, in a totally different context, similar extenuations fade into insignificance against the sin of adultery. In his *Sermo de nupcijs* (*Wedding Sermon*), pp. 291–2, John Mirk (see note 7 above) tells a cautionary tale demonstrating the punishments awaiting those who "brekon þis ordur" of holy matrimony. The tale involves "an olde knythe" who "wedded a ȝung ladi; but for þis olde man plesud not hure alle to lekyng of hur, scheo toke anothur freke knyte þat was neghtbur to hem" (an old knight who married a young lady; but because the old man didn't measure up to her expectations, she took up with a different, rakish knight who was their neighbour). Mirk describes the sudden death of the wife and lover, their subsequent punishments and eventual aid through the prayers of a pious lord. His point is that "þus is weddyng holy in begynnyng" (thus marriage is sacred from the start). The age discrepancy between wife and knight is of interest only as the occasion for sin. Its importance for making the wife's infidelity more understandable and its potential for criticism of age incompatibility within marriage are given no coverage.

12 "Useth", in its specifically sexual sense, also captures the Augustinian distinction between using something as a means to an end and enjoying something as an end in itself. Intercourse should properly be used as the means for procreation rather than as a pleasurable end in itself.

13 Guillaume de Lorris and Jean de Meun, *Le Roman de la Rose*, (begun by Lorris 1230–35; de Meun's continuation *c.* 1268–85), edited by Félix Lecoy, 3 vols, Champion, Paris, 1965, 1966, 1970. (Lorris's section: lines 1–4058; de Meun's section 4059–21780).

14 For example, Aquinas, op. cit., 1a 118 ad 4 (vol. XV): "In the higher animals brought into being through coitus, the active power resides in the male's semen . . . while the material of the foetus is provided by the female." Galen's theory that the female produces semen is neither as popularly accepted as Aristotelian theory in the

mediaeval period, nor as progressive as it might appear. Female
seed, even if present, is considered less active than male seed.

15   This is rather a bold assertion since Larry D. Benson has repudiated
every claim but one for Chaucerian puns on "queynte"; see his
"The 'Queynte' Punnings of Chaucer's Critics" in *Reconstructing
Chaucer*, edited by Paul Strohm and Thomas J. Heffernan, New
Chaucer Society, Knoxville, Tennessee, 1985, pp. 23–47. Benson
argues that "queynte" is an occasional and rare euphemism for
"cunte", being an adjective used as a noun and meaning
approximately "pleasing, elegant thing". He maintains that
usages such as the Wife of Bath's "ye shul have queynte ynogh at
eve" (III 332) alludes not to "cunte" at all but to "sexual activity"
(p. 44). All association between "queynte" and "cunte" is
forbidden because there is no direct etymological relation between
them. While the etymological caveat needs to be made, it seems far
from likely that Chaucer did not intend the word to sound and
mean something enough like "cunte" for the association to be
appreciated. As Benson has argued, Chaucer has already shown
his awareness of the phonological and semantic similarity between
the words (I 3275–6). I suggest that a similar allusion is intended
behind the primary sense of "queynte" as "deceptive" in IV 2061.
There is no grammatical difficulty with this secondary sense of
"sweet venym queynte" as the noun "venym" could be used
adjectivally. See the *Oxford English Dictionary*, second edition,
which records this usage from the mid and late fourteenth and early
fifteenth centuries.

Alison Smith: How William Carlos Williams Gave Birth: pp. 117–33

1   Wallace Stevens wrote an early letter to Williams warning him that
his "incessant new beginnings" would simply "lead to sterility";
Williams however is clearly keen on the possibility of endless
beginnings, births and rebirths in his work. These phrases from
Stevens are quoted from Williams's "Prologue to *Kora in Hell*",
Selected Essays of William Carlos Williams, Random House, New
York, 1954, pp. 3–26.

2   The phrase first appears in a short poem called "Paterson" in 1927.

3   James Fenton, "Poetry Masterclass", "The Sunday Review", *The
Independent on Sunday*, 18th March 1990.

4   J. Hillis Miller, *Criticism in Society* edited by Imre Saluzinszky,
Methuen, London, 1987, p. 233.

5   Bram Dijkstra, quoted from his introduction to *A Recognizable Image:
William Carlos Williams on Art and Artists*, New Directions, New
York, 1978.

6 The 1919 quotation is from "A Maker", *The Little Review*, August 1919, edited by Margaret Anderson and Jane Heap, p. 38; the quotations from *Spring and All* are from *Collected Poems 1909–1939* edited by A. Walton Litz and C. MacGowan, Carcanet, Manchester, 1987, pp. 204 and 219; the quotation beginning "once the writing . . . " is from Williams's short piece "How to Write", reprinted in: *Interviews with William Carlos Williams: "Speaking Straight Ahead"*, edited by Linda Wagner, New Directions, New York, 1976; the 1957 quotation is from a late interview in the last cited text, p. 73.

7 *Collected Poems 1909–1939*, p. 154.

8 Charles Doyle, *William Carlos Williams and the American Poem*, MacMillan, London, 1982, p. 169. Similar discussions can be found in Hillis Miller's *Poets of Reality*, Belknap Press/Harvard University Press, Cambridge, Mass., 1966, pp. 306–7, and Dijkstra's *The Hieroglyphics of a New Speech: Cubism, Stieglitz and the Early Poetry of William Carlos Williams*, Princeton University Press, New Jersey, 1969, p. 132. For brilliant refutation, see Henry M. Sayre's *The Visual Text of William Carlos Williams*, University Press of Illinois, Urbana, 1983.

9 The locality theme is discussed in detail in several critical works on WCW, but very helpfully in Christopher MacGowan's *William Carlos Williams's Early Poetry*, Epping-Bowker, USA, 1984, and Paul Mariani's critical biography, *William Carlos Williams: A New World Naked*, McGraw Hill, New York, 1981.

10 Williams, writing in his *Autobiography*, New Directions, New York, 1967, p. 58.

11 Ezra Pound, letter to Williams, 10th November 1917, *The Letters of Ezra Pound 1907–1941* edited by D.D. Paige, Harcourt, Brace & Co., New York, 1950.

12 Williams, "The American Background", *Selected Essays*, pp. 157–8.

13 Thom Gunn, review of *Collected Poems 1909–1939*, *TLS*, 19th–25th February 1988.

14 *Collected Poems 1909–1939*, p. 129.

15 Williams, letter to Alva N. Turner, 27th February 1921, *Selected Letters of William Carlos Williams* edited by J.C. Thirlwall, McDowell-Oblensky, New York, 1957.

16 Williams, *I Wanted to Write a Poem*, New Directions, New York, 1977.

17 *Little Review*, May 1927.

18 Williams, "The Three Letters", *Contact*, IV, edited by McAlmon and Williams.

19 *Contact*, IV.

20 Williams, *The Great American Novel*, The Three Mountains Press, Paris, 1923, Richard West Reprints, 1980, p. 10.

21 *Collected Poems 1909–1939*, p. 143.

22 Williams, "Shakespeare", *Selected Essays*, p. 55.
23 All quotations following are from this latter August letter, *The Egoist*, August 1917, edited by Harriet Shaw Weaver. Paul Mariani in *William Carlos Williams: A New World Naked* and Mike Weaver in *William Carlos Williams: The American Background*, Cambridge University Press, 1971, only briefly address the issues raised by these letters. Audrey T. Rogers is the author of the only substantial published work on W.C.W. and gender, but her book, *Virgin and Whore: The Image of Women in the Poetry of William Carlos Williams*, McFarland & Co, Jefferson, 1987, concentrates on an equality that she feels Williams attributes to women; in his regard for them she finds "hope for reconciliation and consummation" in response to "the fragmentation, isolation and despair of modern existence" (p. 4). According to Rogers, and in interesting subconscious terms, "few male poets have so eagerly sought to penetrate that mystery [of Woman], and few with such largeness of spirit and imagination" (ibid.).
24 The book was published by the organizer of the exhibition, Samuel Kootz. Williams was responding to a painting called "Women with an Oracle" by Romane Bearden. The essay is reprinted in *A Recognizable Image*.
25 *In the American Grain*, A. and C. Boni, New York, 1925, Penguin, 1989, p. 184.
26 *The Great American Novel*, p. 20.
27 Stevens notes Williams's interest in the "anti-poetic" in his preface to Williams's *Collected Poems* of 1934.
28 *Collected Poems 1909–1939*, p. 40.
29 Ibid., p. 56.
30 Ibid., p. 166–7.
31 *I Wanted to Write a Poem*, p. 14.

Jane Goldman: "Metaphor and Place in *To the Lighthouse*": pp. 139–55

1 Virginia Woolf, *A Room of One's Own*, The Hogarth Press, London, 1929, p. 7.
2 Woolf, *To the Lighthouse*, The Hogarth Press, London, 1927.
3 Thomas Szasz, *Karl Kraus and the Soul-Doctors*, Routledge and Kegan Paul, London, 1977, p. 159.
4 "J'Accuse", *Without Walls*, Channel 4, 29th January 1991.
5 V.N. Voloshinov [M.M. Bakhtin], "Discourse in Life and Discourse in Poetry", translated by J. Richmond, in *Bakhtin School Papers*, edited by Ann Shukman, Russian Poetics in Translation, Oxford, 1983, p. 19.

6   Walter Benjamin, *The Origin of German Tragic Drama*, translated by J. Osborne, New Left Books, London, 1977, pp.178–9.

7   Jacques Derrida, *Margins of Philosophy*, translated by Alan Bass, Harvester Press, Brighton, 1982.

8   Marina Warner, *Monuments and Maidens: the Allegory of the Female Form*, Weidenfeld and Nicolson, London, 1985; Picador, London, 1985, p. xx.

9   For full publication details of *A Room of One's Own* see note 1.

10 Sir Walter Scott, *Minstrelsy of the Scottish Border*, edited by T.F. Henderson, Blackwood, Edinburgh, 1812, vol. 3, p. 370.

11 Scott, op. cit., vol. 3, p. 360.

12 Warner, op. cit., p. 35; she is quoting the first century BC treatise by Vitruvius, *De Architectura*, I, 4, lines 8–15.

13 See *To the Lighthouse* pp. 279 and 285, and Maria DiBattista, "*To the Lighthouse*: Virginia Woolf's Winter's Tale", in *Virginia Woolf: Revaluation and Continuity*, edited by Ralph Freedman, University of California Press, Berkeley, Los Angeles, and London, pp. 161–88.

14 Translation taken from Annabel Patterson's *Pastoral and Ideology: Virgil to Valéry*, Clarendon Press, Oxford, 1987, pp. 50–51.

15 Nec nemorum tantam per secula multa quietem
    Viderat ulla dies: passim saturata iacebant
    Armenta et lenis pastores somnus habebat;
    Pars teretes baculos, pars nectere serta canendo
    Frondea, pars agiles calamos; *tum fusca nitentem*
    Obduxit Phebum nubes, precepsque repente
    Ante expectatum nox affuit; horruit ether
    Grandine terribili; certatim ventus et imber
    Servire et fractis descendere fulmina nimbis,
    Altior, ethereo penitus convulsa fragore,
    Corruit et colles concussit et arva cupressus.
    . . .
    Ingentis strepitu tremefacta ruine.
    Pastorum mox turba fugit, quecunque sub illa
    Per longum secura diem consederat umbra.
    Petrarch, Second Eclogue, lines, 2–13, 19–21, quoted in Patterson, op. cit.; my italics.

16 My Ph.D. thesis offers a Post-Impressionist reading of Woolf's fiction. This differs from the orthodox view of Woolf's response to Post-Impressionism as based on Roger Fry's and Clive Bell's theory of Significant Form, in suggesting an alternative definition based on the handling of light, shade, and colour, as exemplified in the work of Woolf's sister, Vanessa Bell.

17 Samuel Johnson, *A Journey to the Western Islands of Scotland*, London, 1775: reprinted in *Johnson's Journey to the Western Islands of Scotland and Boswell's Journal of a Tour to the Hebrides*, edited by R.W. Chapman, Oxford University Press, London, 1924, p. 9.

18 Peter Womack, *Improvement and Romance: Constructing the Myth of the Highlands*, Macmillan, London, 1989.

19 Womack, pp. 67–8.

20 Woolf, "Charlotte Brontë", in *The Essays of Virginia Woolf, Volume 2, 1912–1918*, edited by Andrew McNeillie, The Hogarth Press, London, 1987, p. 193; *The Letters of Virginia Woolf, Volume 3: A Change of Perspective*, edited by Nigel Nicolson and Joanne Trautmann, The Hogarth Press, London, 1977, p. 389.

21 Woolf, *Letters*, vol. 3, p. 374.

22 Woolf, *Letters*, vol. 3, p. 379.

23 See the unsigned review of *Night and Day* in *The Times Literary Supplement*, 30th October 1919, p. 607.

24 Joan Bennett, *Virginia Woolf, Her Art as a Novelist*, Cambridge University Press, Cambridge, 1945, p. 79.

25 Bennett, op. cit., p. 81.

26 James Hafley, *The Glass Roof*, University of California Press, Berkeley and Los Angeles, 1954, p. 78.

27 David Daiches, *Virginia Woolf*, Poetry London, London, 1945, pp. 76, 81.

28 Daiches, op. cit., p. 81.

29 Daiches, op. cit., p. 76.

30 Ibid.

31 Jean O. Love, *Worlds in Consciousness: Mythopoetic Thought in the Novels of Virginia Woolf*, University of California Press, Berkeley and Los Angeles, California, 1970, p. 70.

32 Woolf, *Moments of Being: Unpublished Autobiographical Writings*, edited by Jeanne Schulkind, Chatto & Windus, London, 1976, p. 90.

33 Sue Roe, *Writing and Gender*, Harvester Wheatsheaf, Hemel Hempstead, 1990, p. 63.

34 M.H. Levenson, *A Genealogy of Modernism*, Cambridge University Press, Cambridge, 1984, pp. 154–5.

35 Woolf, *Mrs. Dalloway*, The Hogarth Press, London, 1925, p. 41.

36 " . . . where'er thy bones are hurled,
    Whether beyond the stormy Hebrides,
    Where thou perhaps under the whelming tide
    Visit'st the bottom of the monstrous world . . . "
    John Milton, "Lycidas", in *Poetical Works of John Milton*, edited by Douglas Bush, Oxford University Press, Oxford, 1966, lines 155–8.

37 For an account, in Gaelic and English, of the disaster, see Tormod Callum MacDonald, *Call na h-Iolaire*, Accair, Stornaway, 1978. Woolf's reference to "the Isles of Stornaway" is in *Letters*, vol. 3, p. 217.

38 See Quentin Bell, *Virginia Woolf: A Biography, Volume 2: Mrs Woolf 1912–1941*, The Hogarth Press, London, 1972, pp. 205–6.

39   The General Strike of 1926, in the midst of which Woolf was writing "Time Passes", suggests another failed rebellion as context.

40   Bishop R. Forbes, *The Lyon in Mourning*, Edinburgh, 1895–6, vol. I, p. 75.

41   Forbes, vol. II, p. 20.

42   Woolf, *To the Lighthouse: The Original Holograph Draft*, edited by S. Dick, The Hogarth Press, London, 1982, p. 220.

43   See for example Madeline Moore, *The Short Season Between Two Silences: The Mystical and the Political in the Novels of Virginia Woolf*, Allen and Unwin, London, 1984, pp. 78–81; Makiko Minow-Pinkney, *Virginia Woolf and the Problem of the Subject*, Harvester Press, Brighton, 1987, p. 101; Rachel Bowlby, *Virginia Woolf: Feminist Destinations*, Basil Blackwell, Oxford, 1988, p. 77.

44   The '45 is not the only Scottish direction in which the name McNab leads us. On a lighter note, we might also consider how John Buchan's novel *John MacNab* (1925) tells the story of three London businessmen on holiday in Scotland who adopt the name "MacNab" as a *nom de guerre* under which they feel free to misbehave without tarnishing their professional reputations. Woolf seems to harbour similar escapist fantasies herself with regard to the Hebrides: from London, where she is working on *To the Lighthouse*, she writes to her lover, Vita Sackville-West: "am I here . . . or in a bedroom up in the Hebrides? I know which I like best – the Hebrides. I should like to be with you in the Hebrides at this moment." *Letters*, vol. 3, p. 244.

Mary Orr: Crossing Divides: *Miss X, or the Wolf Woman*: pp. 156–72

1   Christine Crow, *Miss X, or the Wolf Woman*, The Women's Press, London, 1990. All page references are to this text. The following are the references for reviews to date on *Miss X*:
The Women's Press Bookclub Catalogue, October–December 1990, pp. 3, 9, 13.
The St Andrew's Citizen, 19th October 1990.
Lucy O'Brien, "Xual Healing", *City Limits*, 22nd November 1990.
A. McAdam Clark, "Miss X, or the Wolf Woman", *Rouge*, Winter, 1990–91, p. 42.
Bronwen Grey, *The Beaver*, 3rd December 1990.
The Pink Times, Oxford, Autumn Edition 1990, p. 20.
Time Out, 24.10.90, Lesley Thomson, "Focus".
"The Late Show", BBC 2, 24th September 1991, Sara Maitland on *Miss X* for the alternative Booker List.
Tessa Ransford's top choice of *Miss X* for the Christmas Book List, *The Scotsman*, 7th–8th December 1991.

2 *Rouge*, art. cit.
3 *The Beaver*, art. cit.
4 *City Limits*, art. cit.
5 Judith Butler, *Gender Trouble: Feminism and the Subversion of Identity*,
   Routledge, London, 1990, p. xi. "Phallogocentrism" is a
   combination of two concepts, the Phallus and the Logos, and is a
   term used frequently in feminist criticism to describe the
   imaginary and symbolic representation of the subject as male. This
   is because, in psychoanalytic terms, representation takes place in
   and through language, which has as its Signifier the Phallus. Only
   Man may have this: Woman is positioned as his Other as she
   lacks it. In the history of Western Metaphysics, secondly, the Logos
   imparts a dualistic system on thought and language, the first term
   implying and commanding the second, for example Man: Woman,
   Good: Evil. Derrida sought in Deconstruction to undo this binary
   through his concept of "différance". Many feminist critics regard
   even this move as another guise of the power of the (male) Logos.
6 Toril Moi, *Sexual/Textual Politics*, New Accents Series, Routledge,
   London, 1985.
7 *City Limits*, art. cit.
8 *The Pink Times*, art. cit.
9 "Feminist anti-*Bildungsroman*": a *Bildungsroman* is a novel concerned
   with education and development, often of the (usually male) artist.
10 Lacan describes three main orders, the Imaginary, the Symbolic
   and the Real. Malcolm Bowie's *Lacan* (Fontana Press, 1991)
   succinctly defines the Lacanian Symbolic as "the realm of language,
   the unconscious and an otherness that remains other. This is the
   order in which the subject as distinct from the ego comes into being,
   and into a manner of being that is always disjointed and
   intermittent." (p. 92). The Symbolic order has priority over the
   Imaginary, and some control over the Real, but this latter always
   defines that which lies outside the Imaginary/Symbolic of the
   subject and of the subject's definition in and through language.
11 Harold Bloom, *The Anxiety of Influence*, Oxford University Press,
   Oxford, 1973.
12 *Mise en abyme* is the self-reflexive mirroring of the subject within its
   own work; for example, the writer may be a figure in the text
   itself. This doubling elucidates the deceptions of mimesis and
   emphasizes the ever-retreating hold language and representation
   has on meaning or signification. *Mise en abyme* thus examines that
   which is mirrored and the processes of representation in art itself.

Christine Crow: A Voice Between the Bars?: pp. 173–81

1   fleshers, *butchers*
2   dreich, *dreary*
3   doos, *doves*
4   Ossian: one of Literature's greatest frauds, perpetrated by James
    Macpherson, an eighteenth-century Scottish poet who claimed to
    have discovered and translated the epic poems of an ancient Gaelic
    bard, Ossian. The "translations" received almost hysterical praise
    and won admirers as diverse as Goethe and Napoleon, although
    Dr Johnson was never deceived.
5   The Auld Alliance: the longstanding political and cultural
    connection between France and Scotland.
6   For a translation of the poem, together with the full French text,
    see Grahame Martin's critical edition *Le Cimetière Marin (The
    Graveyard by the Sea)*, Edinburgh Bilingual Library, University of
    Texas Press, Austin, Texas, 1972). I have written about the poem
    myself in *Paul Valéry and the Poetry of Voice*, Cambridge University
    Press, 1982, p. 201–15.
7   See Michèle le Doeuff, "Women and Philosophy" in *French Feminist
    Thought: A Reader*, ed. Toril Moi, Basil Blackwell, Oxford, 1990.
8   A reference to the famous trick drawing of a creature which can be
    seen as either a rabbit or a duck – but can it be seen as both at
    once? See the illustration on page 178.
9   For the use of such terms in contemporary gender theory see
    Margaret Whitford, *Luce Irigaray: Philosophy in the Feminine*, Routledge,
    London, 1990, and *The Irigaray Reader*, ed. Margaret Whitford, Basil
    Blackwell, Oxford, 1991.

Notes on Contributors

Flora Alexander

Flora Alexander is a lecturer in English at the University of
Aberdeen. She studied at Aberdeen and Oxford, and lectured at
the University of Liverpool before her present appointment. She
teaches and researches in the area of twentieth-century fiction,
especially fiction by women. Other strong interests are represented
by her active membership of the British Association for Canadian
Studies and the International Arthurian Society. She is joint co-
ordinator of the Women's Studies course at Aberdeen University,
and handles the English Department's ERASMUS contacts with
German-speaking universities. Her publications include articles
on mediaeval literature, and *Contemporary Women Novelists* (Edward
Arnold, 1989). Her most recent work includes articles on the
Quebec stories of Mavis Gallant, and the idea of the Highlander
in Margaret Laurence's *The Diviners*.

Valerie Allen

Valerie Allen did her Ph.D. at Trinity College Dublin and has
lectured at University College Dublin, Birkbeck College,
University of London and Stirling University where she is currently.
She is presently editing a Casebook on Chaucer's *Canterbury Tales*.

Carol Anderson

Carol Anderson was born in Lahore, Pakistan, and educated at school in Dundee and at the universities of Aberdeen and Edinburgh. She has worked in Japan and Italy, and now teaches Scottish Literature at Glasgow University. She edited Violet Jacob's *Diaries and Letters from India 1895–1900* (Canongate, Edinburgh, 1990). She is also preparing an edition of Jacob's historical novel, *Flemington*, to be published in 1993 by the Association of Scottish Literary Studies.

Christine Crow

Christine Crow came to lecture in Scotland in 1965 after reading Modern Languages at Girton College, Cambridge and studying in Paris as part of her Ph.D. on the poetry and thought of Paul Valéry. She was promoted to a Readership in French Literature in the University of St Andrews in 1979, then gave up her teaching post in 1986 in order to write full-time. Her first novel, *Miss X, or the Wolf Woman* appeared with The Women's Press in 1990, and she was recently a contributor to *Taking Reality by Surprise*, ed. Susan Sellers, The Women's Press, 1991, and *Lines Review*, ed. Tessa Ransford, June 1991. Her previous works include *Paul Valéry, Consciousness and Nature*, Cambridge University Press, 1972, *Paul Valéry and Maxwell's Demon*, University of Hull Publications, 1972, and *Paul Valéry and the Poetry of Voice*, Cambridge University Press, 1982. She is currently Honorary Reader in French and Fellow of St Leonard's College in the University of St Andrews.

Margaret Elphinstone

Margaret Elphinstone is the author of two novels, and, most recently, a book of short stories, *An Apple From a Tree* (1991). She has also published two gardening books, and is the editor of an anthology of garden poetry. She returned to university in 1989 in order to study the development of the Scottish historical novel, and is now a lecturer in English Studies at Strathclyde University. She has two daughters and lives in Edinburgh. She is currently working on her third novel.

Jane Goldman

Jane Goldman was born in Scotland and brought up in South Yorkshire. She lectures in American Literature and Modernism

in the English Department of the University of Edinburgh, where
she is also completing a Ph.D. on Virginia Woolf and Post-
Impressionism. She is a regular visitor to Skye.

Dorothy Porter McMillan

Dorothy Porter McMillan lectures in English Literature at the
University of Glasgow. She has edited Elizabeth Barrett
Browning's *Sonnets from the Portuguese* (William Collins, London,
1969), George Douglas Brown's *The House with the Green Shutters*
(Penguin, Harmondsworth, 1985), and Christine Miller's *A
Childhood in Scotland* (Canongate, Edinburgh, 1989). She reviews
books and theatre for *The Glasgow Herald*. Her recent publications
and current work are on Scottish women's writing, particularly
autobiographical writing.

Mary Orr

Mary Orr has held posts in French at University College, Swansea
and Christ Church, Oxford before taking up a Lectureship in
French at the University of St Andrews. She wrote her Ph.D. thesis
at Cambridge on Intertextuality in the works of Claude Simon
(Nobel Prize Winner for Literature 1985) to be published in revised
form by Glasgow University Press. Her research interests and
published articles range over a variety of fields of French studies:
Romanticism, Flaubert's *Education Sentimentale*, Claude Simon; and
the broader issues of intertextuality, literary translation,
autobiography, critical theory and French feminism. She is also
currently the French Editor for the journal *Forum for Modern
Language Studies*.

Alison Smith

Alison Smith was born in 1962 in Inverness. She was educated at
the University of Aberdeen and at Newnham College, Cambridge.
She now teaches in the English Studies department of the
University of Strathclyde. She is a poet and playwright. Her plays,
The Dance, Trace of Arc, and *Comic*, have been performed at the
Edinburgh Festival Fringe. Whilst at Cambridge she co-directed
the first Women's Footlights Revue, also performed at the Fringe.
Her poetry has been published in *The New Statesman* and in *The
Scotsman*, and in two anthologies, *Original Prints* (Polygon Books,
Edinburgh, 1987), and *An Anthology of Scottish Women Poets*, edited
by Catherine Kerrigan (Edinburgh University Press, Edinburgh,

1991). She has edited *Plays, Poems, and Prose of J.M. Synge* for Everyman (forthcoming, August 1992) and is currently co-editing a book of essays on Scottish writers and Modernism.

Index